PAPAL ANOMALIES AND THEIR IMPLICATIONS

PAPAL
ANOMALIES

AND THEIR IMPLICATIONS

BY STEVEN SPERAY

Cover Art: Pietro Vannucci (1446–1524 A.D.)
"The Giving of the Keys to Saint Peter" (1482 A.D.)
This fresco is located in the fifth compartment in the northern wall of the Sistine Chapel.

Jean-Paul Laurens (1838-1921 A.D.)
"Pope Formosus and Stephen VII (1870 A.D.)
The *"Cadaver Synod"* held in 897 A.D.
Musée des Beaux-Arts, Nantes

The story to the picture is found in the eighth anomaly chapter of this book on page 69.

Cover design and format by Steven Speray

PAPAL ANOMALIES
AND THEIR IMPLICATIONS

Second Edition

Copyright 2011 A.D. by Steven Speray

ISBN: 978-0-578-08139-7

Published by Confiteor
PO BOX 83
Versailles, KY 40383
www.catholictopgun.com

VERITAS

AD MAJOREM DEI GLORIAM

Acknowledgments

I would like to express my gratitude to those that helped me put this book together:

Wayne Yeager. He is an author, successful entrepreneur, and my dearest friend. His knowledge of the internet and practically everything else, except religion, is amazing. It was Wayne who gave me the suggestion of placing pictures in this book, using a serif font, and creating a better cover.

Matthew Haltom. He is a perfectionist and another dear friend. He's constantly harping to me on my poor grammar and encourages me to better my writing. I hope he likes this one.

Hutton Gibson. He is a faithful Catholic and master defender of the Faith. His corrections and suggestions, both historically and grammatically, have helped me realize that I need to pay much closer attention to detail.

Although none of the above has endorsed my book in anyway, I greatly appreciate the help given to me!

The responsibility for this book's content is mine. I offer it to help Catholics and non-Catholics better understand the situation of today's Catholic Church by using the history of the papacy to demonstrate that fact. It is my hope that this work will encourage men to see the truth of the Catholic Church and enter into it.

I would like to make a comment about the cover of this book. *The Giving of the Keys to Saint Peter* by Vannucci is a classic example of Renaissance art. I've never been a fan of it. In *The Transfiguration of Christ,* Rafael, student of Vannucci, depicts Christ as a pregnant woman. Leonardo de Vinci depicts St. John as a woman in his Last Supper. Honestly, I find their art to be quite sacrilegious.

However, my favorite artist of all time is probably Gustave Doré. I use a few of his images on pp. 27, 49, and 111. Not only is his work fantastic, it's very extensive. He has thousands of engravings, sketches, and illustrations. I highly suggest an exploration of his wonderful artwork.

                                        Steven Speray
                                        April 5, 2011 A.D.
                                        Feast of St. Vincent Ferrer

Contents

Introduction..17

First Anomaly: The Interregnum between
St. Marcellinus and St. Marcellus I....................29

Second Anomaly: Is it Liberius
or St. Felix II?...33

Third Anomaly: Dioscorus, an Antipope?..............43

Fourth Anomaly: The Good, the Bad,
and the Ugly...47

Fifth Anomaly: Hazy Honorius...........................53

Sixth Anomaly: St. Martin and St. Eugene...........59

Seventh Anomaly: Pope? Stephen II...................65

Eighth Anomaly: Formosus and His Screwy
Successors..69

Ninth Anomaly: John X, Leo VI, and
Stephen VII
(with Papal Family Dynasty Tree, p. 77)..............73

Tenth Anomaly: John XII, Leo VIII,
and Benedict V..79

Eleventh Anomaly: Benedict VI
and Boniface VII..85

Twelfth Anomaly: The Hodgepodge of Popes
Benedict IX, Sylvester III, Gregory VI,
Clement II, Damasus II, and St. Leo IX................89

Thirteenth Anomaly: Antipope Benedict X...........95

Fourteenth Anomaly: Anacletus II vs.
Innocent II..97

Fifteenth Anomaly: The Long Interregnums
of the Thirteenth and Fourteenth
Centuries...103

Sixteenth Anomaly: Pope? Hadrian V................111

Seventeenth Anomaly: The Mistaken
John XXII...115

Eighteenth Anomaly: The Great Schism............119

Nineteenth Anomaly: Alexander VI
buys the Papacy..129

Twentieth Anomaly: The Great Apostasy..........139

A Summary of Implications: From the Twenty Anomalies..161

Author's List of Popes and Antipopes...............165

Bibliography 177

About the Author...181

PAPAL ANOMALIES AND THEIR IMPLICATIONS

INTRODUCTION

The Catholic papacy may be the most misunderstood doctrine in Christianity. Even some Catholic theologians misunderstand it and therefore misrepresent it. It is very important to understand this doctrine in order to follow the implications in each of the following anomalies.

The papacy is the office of the Catholic Faith, which constitutes the visible Head of Christianity, united to Christ the invisible Head of the Church. Because Christ ever remains the Head of the Church, this divine institution is never headless. The Catholic Church claims the Apostle Peter as being the first Roman Pontiff or pope and having with him successors.

The office must be distinguished from the man holding the office. The pope is addressed as Holy Father or Your Holiness, but these titles are not necessarily describing the pope himself, but the office. In fact, the pope may not be holy at all. Although many have been saintly, it is true that many have also been wicked, even monstrous. I'm sure one of the agonies during the Passion of Our Lord Jesus was visualizing the future of His Church and the devils that would occupy the holy office He established for the good of civilization. How many of those popes have *"spurned the Son of God, and profaned the blood of the covenant by which he was sanctified, and outraged the Spirit of grace,"* and ended up in hell? I'm sure many of the good popes didn't make it straight to heaven either. *"And unto whomsoever much is given, of him much shall be required."* (Luke 12:48)

There is an interesting story about the great Pope Innocent III who appeared on fire in purgatory to St. Lutgarde. The dead pope told the saint that he was supposed to go to hell for a mortal sin but was given the grace of final penitence at death.

The office of the Roman Pontiff is perpetually the head of Christianity, but that doesn't mean there will always be a pope holding the office. The office becomes vacant every time a pope dies, relinquishes the office, loses the faith, becomes schismatic, or becomes doubtful. All of the above are possible, even if it's common to hear *"Catholic"* apologists argue to the contrary. Historically, there have been at least two popes, and perhaps a few more, who have relinquished the office and several have been doubtful. Never has one lost the faith or become schismatic, although this is a possibility.

Whenever the papacy becomes vacant, it is known as an interregnum period. *Sede vacant* means the Chair of Peter is vacant. The pope is ordinarily elected from the College of Cardinals that was constructed and formed from the previous popes. This arrangement has not always been the law. It fact, popes have been elected by the people, forced onto the throne by the emperor, and some were just acknowledged as popes without cause. The current law that cardinals are to elect future popes would not apply under extraordinary circumstances such as the possible extinction of the College of Cardinals. This will be explained later.

Since the head of the household is the man (Ephesians 5, Numbers 1:4), the pope, which means *"papa"*, is the head of the household of God, the Church (Ephesians 2:19-22, I Timothy 3:15). Therefore, the first requirement for the papacy is to be a man. It should be noted that every bishop and priest is *"a"* pope but they are not *"the"* pope. This is why only men can be priests and bishops. Just as the terms king and prince denote men, so too, the very word priest denotes fatherhood.

The pope must have and maintain the Catholic Faith or else he automatically loses the office. This doctrine comes from the universal teaching of all the popes and saints who have ever spoken on the issue, and is supported by canon law, not to mention pure logic. A man cannot be head of the Church, if he is not a member.

The pope is a man like all men; he is a sinful and fallible man. He does not have some special connection with God as if he can hear God directly. He does not necessarily know the Catholic Faith better than the rest of Christianity. The pope is very limited in his authority. He cannot do or teach whatever he wants just because he holds the highest office in the Church. His duty is to guard the truth and teach and preach the Gospel. If necessary, he may expound on the Deposit of Faith by defining or proclaiming a doctrine as part of the Christian Faith. He cannot invent some novel teaching and proclaim it as part of the Christian Faith. It must only come from the Deposit of Faith, which can be seen and understood in light of Holy Scripture and Sacred Tradition.

Sacred Tradition (not to be confused with traditions of men) is a combination of the teaching of Christ and the Apostles, not written down, along with the practice of the Church.

When the pope makes proclamations and definitions as the pope, he is infallible. Infallibility is a special chrism or gift of the pope. It means that the pope cannot err in teaching the faithful under very specific circumstances. When the pope teaches *ex cathedra* (from the Chair) meaning as the head of the whole Church to the whole Church on anything regarding faith and morals to be held as a truth never to be altered, he is infallible. It is a preventive measure given to him by Christ and the Holy Ghost to prevent heresy (known as the *"Gates of Hell"* or *"Powers of Death"*) from ever being taught by the Church.

Just as God used fallible men to write the infallible Holy Scriptures, God now uses fallible men to teach the Gospel of the Holy Scriptures infallibly. The Bible needs some infallible interpretations having boundaries and limits on other interpretations, or else it's every man for himself. The Bible itself was not just assumed to be infallible. The Bible itself is guaranteed by the Catholic Church, which determined its content. Many false writings claim divine inspiration. The Canon of Scripture (books in the Bible) has been infallibly determined by the Church to be infallible. Of course, the Scriptures are infallible if they are God-breathed, but we would not know what precisely which of these God-breathed books are God-breathed without the affirmation of the Church. The Bible was determined and affirmed by Sacred Tradition and the final authority in the Church, the pope. Therefore, without an infallible Church and pope, the Bible itself would not be known, at least, not infallibly.

Besides guarding the Truth, and teaching and proclaiming the Gospel, and defining doctrine, the pope is a symbol of unity. Actually, his office is the symbol of unity since unity can be maintained without a pope. The teaching office, whether vacant or filled, along with all those things that have been previously taught by that office, hold the unity needed for the Church.

The papal office is a justifiable part of true Christianity. In the Gospel of Matthew 16:18-19, we see Christ saying that He will build His Church and then give the keys to the kingdom of heaven to Peter.

The argument whether Peter or Christ is the rock is a moot point. It doesn't really matter. Although historically, every Church father who said anything about this verse, said that it was either Peter and/or Peter's confession of Faith that is the Rock on which Christ built His Church. None said the Rock in this verse was meant to be understood as Christ.

Peter's name obviously means rock, stone, or small pebble, which most probably means that it was about Peter and his faith since this is the context, but again, it doesn't really matter. What matters are the keys to the kingdom.

Christ uses a future tense of the word that He will give Peter the keys sometime in the future. Although, Jesus gives all the Apostles the power to bind and loose in Matt. 18, this should not be confused with the special binding and loosing given specifically to Peter in Matt. 16 after Jesus says that He will give him the keys. This is understood in light of the rest of Holy Writ that speaks of Peter as head of the others.

For instance, Peter is mentioned throughout Holy Scripture as *"Peter and the others"* or some phrase such as this. He also is mentioned in the Holy Bible over one hundred and ninety times. The next closest Apostle most mentioned is John found under thirty times. Peter is clearly understood as one with special significance.

Also, if we turn to Isaiah 22:22, we see that Eli'akim is given the key to the kingdom of David even though Eli'akim is not the king. It is clear that Christ was drawing from this very passage. Jesus is the eternal Son and King and will place under Him one who will be given the keys to the eternal kingdom.

It might be argued that Eli'akim is given a key where as Peter is given keys, therefore, Christ was not drawing-out from the Isaiah passage. I would suggest that such an argument is looking into Holy Scripture anachronistically since the one making the argument is looking for a way out of having to see Peter as the only one holding the keys.

The passage in Isaiah also denotes that the key holder has successors to maintain the authority of keeping in or out of the house or kingdom. Since Jesus was clearly drawing from this image, the intention of Christ is that Peter would have successors with authority of keeping in or out (binding and loosing) of the Church.

One might argue that if the papacy is so important and constitutes what Catholics claim, we would see Christ actually giving Peter the keys in the Holy Bible. The problem with this argument is that the keys represent authority and succession. There is not an actual set of keys. There is no need to see the ceremony, if any, that Peter becomes the actual head of the Church. It is understood.

This brings us to the Council of Jerusalem.

Another argument against Peter's supreme authority is that James appears to be head of the Church at the Council of Jerusalem in the Book of Acts; Chapter 15. This argument most definitely is an anachronistic viewpoint, since there is no reason to believe it. Those who make this argument are the ones trying to look for a reason not to believe Peter is at the helm.

Again, Peter settles the matter after much debate in Acts 15:7. Barnabas and Paul confirm the truth in verse 12 and then James puts in his two-cents worth. James has to say, *"Listen to me"* since his words need everybody's attention unlike Peter's, who already has everybody's attention. Peter does not have to say, *"listen to me"* because they listen and when he spoke, *"the assembly kept silence"* (Acts 15:12). James then gives his judgment on how Peter's words are to be applied.

Again, it is Peter most mentioned in the Book of Acts. *"Peter stood up among the brethren...and said"* (Acts 1:15). *"Peter standing with the eleven, lifted up his voice and addressed them"* (Acts 2:14). *"Peter and the rest of the Apostles"* (Acts 2:37). *"Peter said to them"* (Acts 2:38). *"Peter saw it and addressed the people"* (Acts 3:12). *"Peter, filled with the Holy Spirit, said to them"* (Acts 4:8). *"Peter and the apostles answered"* (Acts 5:29). Peter is mentioned another forty-nine times in the Book of Acts alone. There are other verses to show Peter is the shepherd over Christ's flock but these suffice.

One might ask, *"Where does the Bible say Peter was pope?"*

Pope is a term given the office years later. The office is what we are looking for, not the name of the office. The Church gave the office the name. What we see in the Holy Bible is Peter as the head of the Apostles who alone is given the keys signifying that he has been given special authority and successors. Since the Church is likened as the *"household of God"* then *"pope"* is a very proper title.

Why does Peter describe himself as a fellow elder if he is the head elder? Peter is a fellow elder. Head elder doesn't mean that he is no longer a fellow elder. Also, Peter is simply being humble by not referring to himself as chief. Modern popes also use the phrase *"fellow elders"* in their letters, encyclicals, and exhortations.

Why do we see the Apostles' asking who is the greatest in the kingdom of heaven if Peter is understood to be the greatest? Peter's status in authority is not the same as his status in holiness. Popes may even go to hell. For all we know, John may have been holier than Peter.

The Holy Bible is only one avenue to see the papacy. The other is history. Early Church fathers list Peter and his successors. No other Apostle has a list of successors. Only Peter, because the early Church understood that Peter's line of succession is the only one that really counts since it is his office that makes for the final authority among the elders or bishops of the Church.

As early as the end of the first century, Peter's successor Clement (mentioned in Philippians 4:3 according to historians) wrote letters to the Corinthians as head of the Church telling the Corinthians that they must be united to Rome. Yes, Clement uses the axiom we fellow elders at Rome, but it is understood that Clement is the chief elder as the letter is attributed to him.

The historic facts clearly prove that Peter has been recognized by all of Christianity as the first pope with Linus, Cletus, and Clement as his immediate successors. Peter's line of successors has been recognized by virtually all who claim Christianity until the sixteenth century. There is no logical reason to disbelieve in the papacy as being part of true Christianity, unless, of course, one rejects as did the original Protestants, the two-thousand-year historic understanding of the Church and Christianity.

The papacy is the logical extension to Christ founding His Church. As implied earlier, without the papacy, every man indeed would be for himself. There could never be a final say that would universally be accepted by the whole. There would never be any real doctrinal unity without the papacy.

Finally, the pope does not always call councils as the Emperor Constantine called Nicea. The pope does not always use his authority as he ought, and he doesn't know everything. His knowledge is limited. The pope can be mistaken when not speaking to the whole world as pope on faith and morals, and can be resisted if he commands one to sin. The pope can unjustly anathematize a good Catholic, and when he does such things, the faithful are duty bound to correct him.

However, the faithful must distinguish between the bad or unjust popes from the antipopes. Popes can be wicked and unjust but they cannot be heretics or schismatics. Antipopes are false claimants to the papacy and there have been many in church history. Only one pope can reign at a time. All claimants to the papacy when a true pope is already reigning are antipopes. Antipopes can also reign when no true pope is in office. Antipopes may be Catholic, or they may be heretics, and whatever the case may be, they have no authority whatsoever and are to be rejected.

The way one can determine whether one is a true pope or antipope is first to determine if the claimant holds the Catholic faith whole and inviolate. If he doesn't, then he is not pope. If his election created reasonable doubt, then by that fact alone, he is not pope.

A few decades ago, Catholics were faced with a serious dilemma. They either had to go against their informed Catholic consciences and historic Catholicism, and accept the Second Vatican Council, or reject the papal claimant as an antipope and the new religion of Rome, which would cause them to be labeled as whacko schismatics by literally everyone. The position, chosen by the latter minority, came to be known as sedevacantism. It means that since the death of Pope Pius XII in 1958 A.D. the Chair of Peter has been empty and occupied by an antipope. The last six claimants to the papal throne are men falsely claiming to be true popes. These antipopes might be recognized as heads of state, but they cannot be recognized as heads of the Church.

His Holiness, Pope Pius XII (reigned March 2, 1939 to October 9, 1958 A.D.) was born on March 2, 1876 A.D. as Eugenio Maria Giuseppe Giovanni Pacelli.

On the surface, it would seem almost lunacy to think that there have not been any true popes in over fifty years, especially in light of the fact that the majority of the world has recognized the last six as true popes. Catholics holding to sedevacantism are often accused of pope-sifting meaning that they will freely exercise in determining which pope is a true pope or an antipope based on private judgment what actions and teachings taken by such men claiming to be pope.

At first glance, this accusation seems to have some merit. However, when you zero in on the premise, you'll find that the accusation is an excuse from having to acknowledge the truth on some matter because of the devastating consequences thereof. In other words, just follow the crowd and believe everything the majority holds regardless what the truth really is. The fact is the majority doesn't necessarily make right or valid as history has presented. There are many arguments used against the position of sedevacantism that have already been debunked by actual historic papal facts.

For instance, there is a common argument used against sedevacantism that claims that a true pope in the future is impossible since the cardinals have become extinct. Thus, the First Vatican Council's declaration of perpetual succession to the papacy would be proved erroneous, an impossible scenario according to Catholic theology. However, cardinals are not absolutely necessary for valid elections (see pp. 109-110), and historic precedents give us recognized true popes who were unlawfully elected. As a matter of fact, there are valid popes who were never elected at all. Therefore, valid popes don't have to be lawfully elected, thus the antisedevacanter's argument is false. Provided that the pope-elect is a man with correct intentions, he can be unlawfully elected, unless there is a specific clause stating otherwise. Even then, it appears one can still be pope.

Case in point, the required consent formula is prescribed. Should the man elected refuse it or to take the papal oath, his election is annulled. *"On the Profession of the Supreme Pontiff"* decreed at the Council of Florence, Session 23, March 26,1436 A.D. stated, *"that the person elected as pope is obliged to express his consent to the election...he is bound to act within a day of the demand. If he does not do so, his election is annulled and the cardinals must proceed in the Lord's name to another election."*

The form of consent is given after these statements which is the required expression of consent needed. Therefore, if one is unlawfully elected because he refused the papal oath, his election would be annulled. Unlawful elections and clauses such as the papal oath have simply gone unnoticed by the experts in pseudo-Catholic apologetics trying to debunk sedevacantism.

Within these pseudo-Catholic circles, are famous contemporary *"Catholic"* historians who are apt to retelling papal history anachronistically as they fit it into their particular viewpoint of theology. They tend to gloss over the grisly and contradictory happenings leading to a dishonest perspective on the papacy.

Adversely, in *"The Decline and Fall of the Roman Church,"* the late Catholic priest, Father Malachi Martin, pulled no punches when he recounted the barbaric and ridiculous affairs of the Catholic papacy. His book is a real gem and unfortunately now out of print and almost forgotten. Some of Fr. Malachi's stories will be retold here. The great Italian *supreme* poet, Dante, provides us with a healthy dose of understanding of the papacy in his *"Divine Comedy"* as well. He included twenty-two popes in his literary classic.

Dante Alighieri (left) by French artist, (right) Gustave Doré (1832 – 1883 A.D.)

Papal history is filled with the bizarre. Popes have nearly destroyed the papacy and the Christian faith in general. As a matter of fact, the history of the papacy is so anomalous that much of it is still unclear. What does it mean for the Catholic Church? That is the question that will be answered here.

This study will include such papal anomalies as how popes recognized by the Catholic Church have been elected while other true popes lived. Impossible, you say? It happened. The Church once recognized an antipope as a true pope for over a thousand years only to be removed from the official list in the twentieth century. The Church has even confused the antipope and the true pope who reigned at the same time and concession has still not been made. Popes have murdered and tortured other popes and what's more, there has even been a family dynasty of popes.

Who were these popes and antipopes and how it all occurred will be presented in a nutshell. The findings are interesting but the conclusions and implications are astounding. They leave behind historic precedents that destroy the modernist pseudo-Catholic beliefs about the papacy. Of course, the true Catholic faith is not in the papacy, but rather in Christ. In other words, the belief and understanding of the papacy comes from Christ first, not vice-versa. Unfortunately, this is confused by many who call themselves Catholic.

Whether you are a Catholic or a non-Catholic, this presentation will leave you thunderstruck. You will never see the papacy the same way again. The following stories can get a little confusing, so stay on your toes and pay close attention. As always with my writings, this work will not be professionally edited. All documentation for the twentieth anomaly can be found in my book, *"The Greatest Conspiracy Ever."* I don't claim to be infallible and therefore don't claim my work to be without error. If any part is contrary to the Faith, I humbly submit to the Church. Throughout this book, I include the rarely seen A.D. (*Anno Domini*, In the Year of Our Lord) after each dated year to remind us of God's sovereignty.

First Anomaly:

The Interregnum between St. Marcellinus and St. Marcellus I

Under the Roman Emperor Nero, the first pope and Apostle St. Peter was put to death upside down on a cross, St. Paul was beheaded, and St. Bartholomew was skinned alive. The Apostles' Sts. James the Less and Matthias were martyred under the reign of Emperor Claudius.

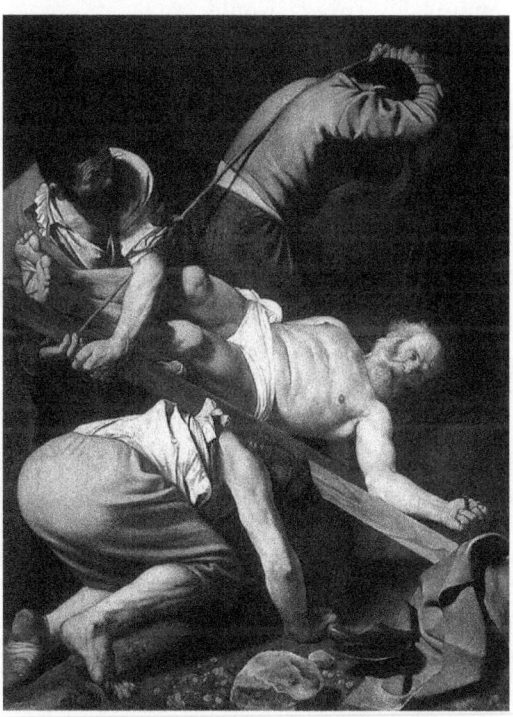

"The Crucifixion of St. Peter" by Michelangelo Merisi da Caravaggio (1600 A.D.)

Under Emperor Trajan, Peter's third successor to the papacy, Pope St. Clement I, was drowned by having an anchor tied around his neck and thrown overboard a Roman warship. Peter's fifth successor, Pope St. Alexander I, was also martyred by beheading under the rule of Trajan.

Popes St. Fabian and Pope St. Cornelius were martyred under Emperor Decius and Pope St. Sixtus II and his companions were put to death by Emperor Valerian. To be a notable Christian or elected pope was like having your death warrant signed.

Deacon St. Lawrence was burned slowly over a fire under Emperor Gallienus and St. Valentine was martyred under Emperor Claudius II. Things would only get worse from there. When Diocletian ascended the throne of the Roman Empire in 284 A.D., many more Catholics were martyred for their faith in Christ Jesus. Times were extremely bloody under the persecutions instigated by Emperor Diocletian. His reign was the longest and severest of all the Roman Emperors.

An apparent victim of this reign of terror was Pope St. Marcellinus who, it is rumored, was executed in 304 A.D. Because Christians feared more reprisals, and probably serving as an imperial reminder of what living Christians were up against, the pope's decapitated body laid on a street in Rome for twenty-six days before being buried by a priest.

Because of the internal divisions within the Church caused by the Roman persecution, the Holy See remained vacant. After the abdication of Diocletian in 305 A.D., the Church suffered fewer persecutions under the new Emperor Maxentius. Less harassed, the Church finally elected Marcellus to the papacy in 308 A.D. The rough and tough God-fearing pope, however, faced his own run-in with the new imperial regime because his rigorism caused an uprising. Maxentius subsequently sent him into exile where he died.

The Implications

The Roman Catholic Church went three and half years without a pope, thus did the Church continue unified in faith and remained the visible Body of Christ despite being driven underground through severe persecution. It is quite obvious that the law of perpetual succession, as dogmatized by the First Vatican Council, cannot mean that the Catholic Church will always have a reigning pope on the Chair of Peter. Therefore, the law of perpetual succession remains with the absence of a pope until the election of the next pope since the limit to an interregnum has never been defined.

In other words, the perpetual principle and visible foundation remains without a pope during long interregnums even when the Church is underground. The Church is not some headless monster during long interregnums. The Church is visibly headless each time a pope dies, but it always has Christ as Her Head. Thus, the Catholic Church remains visible nonetheless.

An interesting note of fact: During the time of Pope St. Marcellinus and St. Marcellus I, all Christians believed in the papacy, seven sacraments, purgatory, etc, as these were the Sacred Traditions of Christ handed down by the Apostles that we are to hold fast to (Second Thessalonians 2:15). The Holy Bible itself would not exist until around 380 A.D. when the Catholic Church fixed the Canon of the Holy Scripture. The idea that all a Christian needs to do is accept Christ as his personal Lord and Savior came many centuries later becoming a fictional man-made tradition that actually nullifies the Word of God, since it contradicts the teachings of Christ as a whole.

Second Anomaly:

Is it Liberius or Felix II?

Before the advent of Emperor Constantine, the Catholic Church and her thirty-two popes were severely persecuted by the Roman Empire. The signing of the Edict of Milan in 313 A.D. by Emperors Galerius, Licinius, and Constantine would forever change the landscape of the Catholic papacy. A new day had dawned for the Church. After Constantine defeated Maxentius at the Milvian Bridge on October 28, 312 A.D., he would enter Rome triumphantly to present to Pope Miltiades, the only black-skinned pope ever to reign over the Church, the Empress Fausta's palace on Monte Celio which became the Lateran palace and the pope's new residence.

Because of the newfound freedom enjoyed by the Church, Pope Miltiades called a council at his new palace to deal with the heretic Donatus in 313 A.D. Councils were not seen since the Council of Jerusalem under the Apostle St. Peter because of the persecution. However, the emperor thought of himself as the head of the Church and the faithful weren't sure if he did or did not have this power. Not satisfied with Rome's council, Constantine called another council at Arles on August 1, 314 A.D. which confirmed Miltiades' declaration against Donatism.

When Bishop Arius declared Christ to be without divinity, Constantine called the First Ecumenical Council at Nicaea in 325 A.D. to answer the heretical bishop. Two particular bishops sharply denounced Arianism. First was the great St. Nicholas who answered Arius himself at the council with a straight-right punch to the nose, which landed him in prison per order of the emperor. The second denunciation of Arianism would come a few years after the council by St. Athanasius.

Icon of Saint Athanasius

Arian theology would gain ground with the bishops of the Church until over ninety percent of the apostolic sees became Arian. A clash of a different kind was about to begin between the pope and the emperor. This time, it was about which of the two controlled the Church at large.

The pro-Arian Emperor Constantius II feared the influence that St. Athanasius, the great defender of the Christian Faith, had against the prodigious Arian heresy. To destroy his credibility, the emperor saw to it that the saint was anathematized by many of the bishops at three different councils. Of course, he wouldn't be satisfied until Pope Liberius joined him in anathematizing St. Athanasius thus confirming the legitimacy of Arianism.

Pope Liberius (reigned 352-366 A.D. and the first pope not recognized as a saint) was a staunch defender of St. Athanasius and the Faith. With bribery and threats, Liberius would not capitulate to the emperor's bullying and in 355 A.D., he banished the pope to Beroea in Thrace.

This would not be the last time a showdown would take place between the pope and the emperor. Such power struggles would continue to reappear as the centuries passed.

When the clergy elected St. Felix in Liberius' place, the unhappy Romans protested and demanded that their pope be returned from exile. However, the government continued to recognize St. Felix, as did many supporters, including clergy. Under the pressure of having St. Felix acting as pope, Liberius appeared to have submitted to Constantius and signed the decrees and condemned St. Athanasius in 357 A.D. St. Jerome wrote how the pope yielded to the Arians in the preface to the *"Liber Precum."*

St. Athanasius would write (357 A.D.), *"Liberius, having been exiled, gave in after two years, and, in fear of the death with which he was threatened, signed [the condemnation of Athanasius]... If he did not endure the tribulation to the end yet he remained in his exile for two years knowing the conspiracy against me."*

Satisfied with the act, the emperor sent Liberius back to Rome to bring peace back to the city on the condition that Liberius and St. Felix rule together.

Speaking on the condemnation of St Athanasius, St. Hilary of Poiters, writing at Constantinople in 360 A.D., addresses Constantius thus: *"I know not whether it was with greater impiety that you exiled him than that you restored him."*

Exhilarated on the return of Liberius, the people shouted *"one God, one Christ, one bishop"* and banished St. Felix to the suburbs.

St. Jerome wrote, *"Liberius conquered by the tedium of exile and subscribing to heretical wickedness entered Rome in triumph."*

Liberius would occupy and rule at the Lateran and St. Felix established a large following of suburbanites of his own. While the majority of the people followed Liberius, nearly all of the clergy followed St. Felix.

Pope St. Anastasius I explained in his epistle *Dat mihi plurimum*, approximately 400 A.D.: *"For at this time when Constantius of holy memory held the world as victor, the heretical African faction was not able by any deception to introduce its baseness because, as we believe, our God provided that the holy and untarnished faith be not contaminated through any vicious blasphemy of slanderous men... For this faith those who were then esteemed as holy bishops gladly endured exile, that is Dionysius, thus a servant of God, prepared by divine instruction, or those following his example of holy recollection, Liberius bishop of the Roman Church, Eusebius also of Vercelli, Hilary of the Gauls, to say nothing of many, on whose decision the choice could rest to be fastened to the cross rather than blaspheme God Christ, which the Arian heresy compelled, or call the Son of God, God Christ, a creature of the Lord."*

St. Felix is recognized in the *Annuario Pontificio* (official list of popes), and the *Liber Pontificalis* (The Book of Popes) paints him as a courageous defender of the Nicene faith, laying his life down for it, while Liberius goes down in history as a weakling, giving in to heresy by accepting the ambiguous First Creed of Sirmium, that omits the Nicene's *"consubstantial with the Father,"* and for excommunicating St. Athanasius. After the death of the Emperor, he recanted everything and attempted to make amends for his wrongdoing.

The *Liber Pontificalis* is an early Christian book that presents brief but detailed biographies of the Roman Pontiffs. It's had varied authors over the centuries and different editions can be found. The *Liber Pontificalis* has been an invaluable part of our knowledge of who's who in the papacy.

The Catholic Encyclopedia calls Pope St. Felix II as *"more properly Antipope."*

Years later, St. Robert Bellarmine would comment on the event: *"Then two years later came the lapse of Liberius, of which we have spoken above. Then indeed the Roman clergy, stripping Liberius of his pontifical dignity, went over to Felix, whom they knew to be a Catholic. From that time, Felix began to be the true Pontiff. For although Liberius was not a heretic, nevertheless he was considered one, on account of the peace he made with the Arians, and by that presumption the pontificate could rightly be taken from him: for men are not bound, or able to read hearts; but when they see that someone is a heretic by his external works, they judge him to be a heretic pure and simple, and condemn him as a heretic."* (St. *De Romano Pontifice*, lib, IV, c. 9, no. 15)

Several popes made comments on the incident.

Pope Pius VI, *Charitas* (# 14), April 13, 1791 A.D.: *"Perhaps in appreciation of these actions, the bishop of Lidda, Jean Joseph Gobel, was elected Archbishop of Paris, while the archbishop was still living. He is following the example of Ischyras, who was proclaimed bishop of Alexandria at the Council of Tyre as payment for his sinful service in accusing St. Athanasius and ejecting him from his See."*

Pope Pius IX, *Quartus Supra* (# 16), January 6, 1873 A.D., On False Accusations: *"And previously the Arians falsely accused Liberius, also Our predecessor, to the Emperor Constantine, because Liberius refused to condemn St. Athanasius, Bishop of Alexandria, and refused to support their heresy."*

Pope Benedict XV, *Principi Apostolorum Petro* (# 3), October 5, 1920 A.D.: *"Indeed, lest they should prove faithless from their duty, some went fearlessly into exile, as did Liberius and Silverius and Martinus."*

The Implications

No doubt, St. Felix started off as an antipope since his election preceded the fall of Pope Liberius. The question is: Did Pope Liberius actually lose his pontificate?

If Liberius was publicly seen or understood to be under real duress when signing the false creed he would not have lost his papacy. However, if Liberius freely signed the Creed or did so secretly under duress, he would have lost his papacy for the appearance of heresy in his weakness in pleasing man rather than God. Thus, after the signature, St. Felix would have become the true pope making Liberius an antipope.

Under the circumstances, Liberius became a doubtful pope after his signature since his orthodoxy would be in question. A doubtful pope is the equivalent to an antipope or vacancy (no pope at all) since there would always be a doubt to his acts. There cannot be a doubtful pope for there cannot be any doubt about any authoritative papal act.

On the flip-side of the coin, St. Felix could not be considered malicious or a formal schismatic for his initial election since the Church was apparently ignorant on the Divine laws of God that under no circumstance can a pope be elected while another pope reigns. After all, he is a saint and he was recognized as a true pope by the Church.

Where does this leave Liberius?

Since he was at best a doubtful pope, he would have automatically lost his office making St. Felix a true pope regardless whether Liberius was innocent or guilty. Of course, this would imply that a pope can be unlawfully elected, since St. Felix first reigned as an antipope.

St. Robert Bellarmine says Liberius was not a heretic but appeared to be which gave the justification for his ousting of the papacy to make room for the reign of St. Felix. In other words, it was right that Catholics recognized Liberius as a heretic and an antipope because he externally appeared to be a heretic even though he was not actually a heretic.

Therefore, the argument that a pope must get a hearing before getting ousted from the papacy is false for it doesn't even take an actual heresy to stop recognizing a true pope if he appears to be a heretic.

If this is the case for true popes, then by logical extension it would apply for cardinals before the election to the papacy. This is the reason why Pope Paul IV in his apostolic constitution *Cum ex Apostolatus Officio* called for the nullity of any papal election of a heretic regardless if all the cardinals recognize the validity of it. This teaching is the Divine law of God and can never be abrogated.

If one rejects St. Bellarmine by not accepting that Liberius was justly recognized as an antipope with the election of St. Felix, then St. Felix should be considered an antipope, or else he must be considered a true pope who was unlawfully elected. However, St. Felix is on the official list of true popes, thus being recognized as a true pope of the Catholic Church.

The case of Pope St. Marcellinus from the first anomaly illustrates an interesting point on this subject in relation to the later popes Liberius and St. Felix.

Based on the lost text of *"Passio Marcellini"* (*The Passion of Marcellinus, also* called *Acts of St. Marcellinus*), Pope Marcellinus, living under the persecution of Diocletian, was called upon to offer an incense sacrifice to the Roman idols. He repented and confessed his faith in Christ only to suffer martyrdom with his companions.

Later, in the fifth century, the Donatist Bishop Petilianus of Constantine claimed in a letter that St. Marcellinus and his priests Melchiades, Marcellus, and Sylvester (his papal successors) had given up the sacred books, and offered incense to the pagan gods. In doing so, these men saved their lives.

It was never proven, but because of these acts, Marcellinus, in his day, was considered to have lost his papacy. He wasn't universally acknowledged as a pope. Some other documents even explain a defection from the pope. The Formula of Hormisdas in 519 A.D. from the East specifically states that *"in the Apostolic See the Church has been preserved without blemish."* Either the Eastern Patriarchs didn't believe the acts ever occurred; they didn't think his acts constituted a blemish on the papacy; or they didn't recognize Marcellinus as a true pope.

St. Augustine appears to have demonstrated that the whole event never happened. However, he did so to protect the papacy presuming (falsely so) that such acts would indeed entail the loss of the papacy even when done under duress as in the case of Marcellinus.

The *Roman Breviary* reads on April 5, *"During the cruel persecution of the Emperor Diocletian, Marcellinus of Rome, overcome with terror, offered incense to the idols of the gods. For this sin he did penance, and wearing a hairshirt, went to the Council of Sinuesso, where many Bishops had assembled, and there he openly confessed his crime."*

Presuming the acts occurred, they wouldn't have constituted the loss of the papacy since they were clearly done under duress at the time and affirmed with the confession of Marcellinus, unlike Liberius which couldn't be known. The point is that we have a precedent in history that demonstrates that acts of apostasy even if they never happened but only appeared so would cause a pope to automatically lose his office. We're not certain the *"Passio"* was presenting actual historic facts, but it doesn't matter. Even a myth can present the truth.

The reason why the pope cannot appear to apostatize from the Faith boils down to the fact that the Catholic Church cannot be led by a doubtful pope.

Reverend Francis X Doyle, S.J. (1927 A.D.) explains: *"The Church is a visible society with a visible Ruler. If there can be any doubt about who that visible Ruler is, he is not visible, and hence, where there is any doubt about whether a person has been legitimately elected Pope, that doubt must be removed before he can become the visible head of Christ's Church. Blessed Bellarmine, S.J., says: 'A doubtful Pope must be considered as not Pope'; and Suarez, S.J., says: 'At the time of the Council of Constance there were three men claiming to be Pope.... Hence, it could have been that not one of them was the true Pope, and in that case, there was no Pope at all....'"*

In light of this teaching, a doubtful pope would lead to doubtful cardinals, which in turn would lead to more doubtful popes through doubtful elections.

In summary, the Church cannot have a doubtful pope. Thus, the pope cannot appear to be a heretic lest he lose his papacy by the judgment of the faithful in the external forum.

The reason why today's Catholic *"sedevacantists"* have not elected a pope over the long interregnum is due to the fact that the problem of having all doubt removed from a future election has not been solved. Perhaps, I should say resolved since the factions of today's Catholics keep aloof a solid election.

I should note that the *Annuario Pontificio* technically is not an official Catholic document. It isn't authoritative and binding to Christians. It was at one time considered official by many of the faithful, but never has the Catholic Church defined who has reigned as Roman Pontiffs.

Also, the term *"Church"* will have different connotations throughout this study. In one sense, it will mean the pope, bishops, etc. in an official capacity. In another sense, it will mean the faithful in general in an unofficial capacity. This distinction is important because the Church in its official capacity cannot lead the faithful astray from salvation. However, unofficially, the Church can err in many other ways that do not pertain to salvation as demonstrated in the following anomalies.

Third Anomaly:

Dioscorus, an Antipope?

On his deathbed in 530 A.D. in an unprecedented act, Pope Felix IV had designated his trusted friend and adviser, Archdeacon Boniface, as his successor to the papacy. However, after Felix's death, the vast majority of the Roman clergy; sixty out of seventy priests and the senate rejected the designation as unconstitutional and refused to acknowledge Boniface as the pope.

Deacon Dioscorus, ex-papal legate under Pope Hormisdas and head of the Byzantine party, was lawfully elected and consecrated by a large majority at the election held at the Lateran basilica.

In no way deterred by this lawful election however, a minority of electors, meeting in the hall of the Lateran Palace, elected Boniface anyway and consecrated him on the same day. Schism then ensued but it was short-lived: Dioscorus died twenty-two days later.

Not to be outdone and upon Dioscorus' death, Boniface II didn't procrastinate in intimidating the sixty presbyters who favored Dioscorus, to retract and condemn Dioscorus' memory, at a synod at Rome in December 530 A.D., and to sign a decree of anathema of their erstwhile pope. After all, asking prayers for the poor soul of Dioscorus would be a humble and Christ-like gesture, and that would be asking too much from one who would do anything to be recognized as the all-powerful Vicar of Christ. Fortunately, a future pope would be more Christ-like and denounce the nonsense of Boniface. The Servant of Servants of God, Pope St. Agapetus I, had the document of condemnation solemnly burned in St. Peter's in 535 A.D.

Dioscorus is not named in the *"official"* list of popes and is considered an antipope.

Dionysius Exiguus (also known as *"Denis the Short,"* lived 470 - 544 A.D.) created the *Anno Domini* dating system. He was a Scythian abbot of a monastery near Rome.

The Implications

Papal designations were not unheard in later papal history. In 531 A.D., Pope Boniface II issued a decree empowering him to choose his own successor. When he chose Vigilius, there was such uproar by the people that Boniface rescinded his nomination and burned the decree. In 1085 A.D., Pope St. Gregory VII chose Blessed Victor III as his successor, who in turn, chose Blessed Urban II in 1086 A.D., who in turn, chose Paschal II in 1099 A.D. These were mere nominations.

It appears that Pope St. Agapetus recognized Dioscorus as a true pope since he refused to have him anathematized, unless, he thought Dioscorus was in error not worthy of anathema, but indeed an antipope.

The election of Boniface II was unlawful at the time regardless of the designation of Pope Felix IV. Therefore, Dioscorus was the legitimate pope, which would have necessarily made Boniface II an antipope. Boniface could have been recognized as a true pope after the death Dioscorus. Boniface is on the official list of true popes, thus being recognized as a true pope of the Catholic Church. Dioscorus has long been considered to be an antipope. However, this is incorrect.

Several implications come from this little niche of papal history. First, the Church did not know for sure if a true pope had the authority to designate his own successor without making a law for it. The definition on papal authority at the First Vatican Council seems to teach that the pope would have the authority to elect his successor. Since the definition comes thirteen-hundred years after the incident, it would not be binding on those of prior centuries. However, Felix had not decreed any new law on the subject, so his designation was meaningless as far as the election for his immediate successor was concerned. The fact remains that back in the sixth century the law was on the side of Dioscorus and not Boniface.

Secondly, the Church didn't recognize a true pope. The *Annuario Pontificio* should have Dioscorus listed as a true pope. The list is clearly not infallible since it has been altered over the years.

Fourth Anomaly:

The Good, the Bad, and the Ugly

Alien to the modern mind is the belief commonly found with Christians in the Middle Ages that God's side always wins in battle. Light overcomes the darkness; good triumphs over evil; truth perseveres over error...always! When the odds are stacked up against the righteous Christian, he will conquer regardless. This attitude would be played out again and again. It was instrumental in the success of the first and second crusades when Christian soldiers traveled long distances enduring bad weather, fatigue, hunger, and sickness, yet defeated the greater number of Muslims. The belief that God's side always prevails was an invaluable part of many other Christian victories over the infidels. It also belonged to the realm of emperors against popes, and popes verses antipopes. Whichever side was right with God would rightly rule the Church; so it was believed.

When Empress Theodora failed in winning over Pope St. Silverius (who reigned from 536 to 537 A.D., previously married, and son of Pope Hormisdas) to the monophysites, she conspired against him with a plot to make him appear to be treasonous against Rome and the Church.

With the takeover of Rome by desecration to churches and catacombs from Ostrogothic King Vitiges, Byzantine General Belisarius secured Rome and conspired with Theodora against Silverius. In a forged letter, Silverius was said to have planned with Vitiges to take over the city by allowing a city gate to remain open.

Peter the Hermit Preaching to the Crusaders
by Gustave Doré

St. Silverius was stripped and wrongly exiled to the island of Palmarola in the Bay of Naples. Vigilius was subsequently consecrated pope in his place. Pope St. Silverius was proved innocent and returned only to find Vigilius had replaced him, who, in turn, with the help of Theodora and Belisarius, exiled him again to the island where he endured extreme hardship and died. St. Silverius is venerated as a saint and is listed in the Roman Martyrology.

Vigilius continued to reign until his death in 555 A.D. He confirmed the Fifth Ecumenical Synod (known as The Second Council of Constantinople of 553 A.D.) and condemned the *Three Chapters*, and leveled nine Canons against Origen.

Immediately after the death of Vigilius, Pelagius was forced onto the Chair of Peter by Emperor Justinian without an election. His consecration was delayed for a year because no bishop would recognize him until two bishops finally came forth to officiate at the ceremony. The reign of Pelagius I lasted from his consecration on April 16, 556 A.D. to his death March 3, 561 A.D.

The Implications

Had Pope St. Silverius actually done what he was falsely accused of; such an action would not cause a pope to lose his office. See page 62 for the explanation why neither Empress Theodora nor the clergy can depose a pope for a crime without violating the Divine law.

Therefore, St. Silverius was the true pope until his death regardless, making Vigilius the antipope. Vigilius (reigned 537-555 A.D.) was acknowledged by all of the Church as the pope after the death of Pope St. Silverius. Thus, his ascent to the throne was unlawful and unjust.

If Vigilius were actually an antipope due to his unlawful ascent and despite mere universal recognition as pope, his confirmation of the Second Council of Constantinople would be null and void until the future true pope accepted its decrees.

However, if Vigilius truly became the pope as recognized by the Church, the implication would be that it is possible for a man to ascend to the Chair of Peter unlawfully and unjustly. Outside of the fact that St. Silverius was invalidly deposed, if no other law prohibited the recognition of an unlawfully elected person to be considered a true pope, universal recognition may prove Vigilius a true pope after Pope St. Silverius' death. Supplied jurisdiction would be given by the Church to one unlawfully elected to keep the Church at bay. In other words, in order to maintain the promise of Christ that the gates of hell won't prevail.

The question is: What is the mechanism that makes the universal recognition the determining factor in making a pope, and at what point? Everybody just *assumes* Vigilius is the true pope because he is recognized by all. Is the mechanism and point in time simply the universal assumption at the death of St. Silverius?

Can a true pope be validly ousted from the papacy by way of conspiracy initiated by the state with the recognition from the Church? Absolutely not! Again, see page 62.

As for Pope Pelagius, a pope need not be elected at all to be considered a true pope. This is an astounding fact in regard to the papacy. However, his recognition as a true pope without an election would explain, to some extent, how it is possible that antipopes, such a Boniface and Vigilius, could become true popes without valid elections.

Is it possible that Boniface, Vigilius and Pelagius were never true popes? If so, the implication would be that the Second Council of Constantinople would be null and void until a future pope recognizes it. If the teachings at the council are subsequently and repeatedly taught, then those teachings from the council would be infallible but the council itself would not be.

If the Fifth Ecumenical Synod is assumed valid because Vigilius is assumed the pope when the assumptions are false, then the implication would be that the Church has erroneously held an invalid pope and council as true. This is certainly a possibility, provided that the council embraced no errors which it apparently didn't since Pope St. Gregory the Great had taught that the council must be upheld and believed.

The Church has already falsely recognized popes as antipopes and antipopes as popes. Therefore, the Church could possibly err in determining what council is officially ratified provided that the council was orthodox.

Such cases would not undermine the doctrine of infallibility, because infallibility only concerns doctrines, disciplines, and laws to be held without error or fault.

Infallibility means spotless or without error, and the Church specifically understands it as exemption or immunity from liability to error or failure. The Church is not infallible outside the realm of doctrine, universal disciplines, and laws. Therefore, the Church may err in government, science, and even within the religion itself, such as personal excommunications, translation of bishops, nominations for the cardinalate, papal letters to individual bishops, priests, or dioceses, etc., and who may be demonically possessed and who may be mentally ill.

Not to be confused with immutability, which means unchangeable, universal disciplines and laws may change, although they are infallible also; such is the teaching of many popes and Church approved theologians. See page 66 for examples.

Infallible doctrines or dogmas can never change. They are set in stone, so to speak.

Fifth Anomaly:

Hazy Honorius

Pope Honorius I was elected pope October 27, 625 A.D. Nine years later, in a reply, *Scripta fraternitatis vestrae*, to Sergius I, patriarch of Constantinople, he wrote, *"Hence, we confess one will of our Lord Jesus Christ."* Thus, he confirmed the heresy of monothelitism.

In the same year of 634 A.D., Honorius again wrote to Sergius in *Scripta dilectissimi filii* that there was only one operation in Christ.

When explaining the one-operation teaching of Honorius, Pope John IV says Honorius was implying that Christ did not have two contrary wills and that both wills of Christ are united, thus forming one operation.

Pope John IV in *Dominus qui dixit* to Emperor Constantius, 641 A.D.: *"...So, my aforementioned predecessor [Honorius] said concerning the mystery of the incarnation of Christ, that there were not in Him, as in us sinners, contrary wills of mind and flesh; and certain ones converting this to their own meaning, suspected that he taught one will of His divinity and humanity which is altogether contrary to the truth."*

Pope John IV is defending Honorius by explaining that he didn't teach monothelitism, which is the doctrine that Christ has only one will. Rather, Honorius, according to John, was teaching that, indeed, Christ had two wills, but they were not working against each other.

Pope St. Martin I condemned monothelitism at the Lataran Council in 649 A.D. with two specific canons.

Canon 10: *"If anyone does not properly and truly confess according to the holy Fathers two wills of one and the same Christ our God...let him be condemned."*

Canon 11: *"If anyone does not properly and truly confess according to the holy Fathers two operations of one and the same Christ our God uninterruptedly united, divine and human, from this that through each of His natures He naturally is the same operator of our salvation, let him be condemned."*

Pope St. Agatho at the Third Council of Constantinople (680 A.D.) apparently did not interpret Honorius as did Pope John IV, for he condemned Pope Honorius as a heretic and an instrument of Satan. However, St. Agatho died before it was ratified.

In 682 A.D., Pope St. Leo II at the 13th session of the Council finally condemns and excommunicates Honorius. *"Also Honorius, who was shown to be incapable of enlightening this Apostolic Church by the doctrine of Apostolic Tradition, in that he allowed its immaculate faith to be blemished by a sacrilegious betrayal."*

Pope St. Leo condemns Honorius not for heresy but for allowing it.

Third Council of Constantinople, Exposition of Faith, 680-681 A.D. stated: *"... the contriver of evil did not rest, finding an accomplice in the serpent and through him bringing upon human nature the poised dart of death, so now too he has found instruments suited to his own purpose – namely, Theodore... Sergius, Pyrrhus, Paul and Peter... and further Honorius, who was pope of elder Rome, Cyrus... and Macarius... - and has not been idle in raising through them obstacles of error against the full body of the Church, sowing with novel speech among the orthodox people the heresy of a single will and a single principle of action..."*

The Third Council of Constantinople, Anonymous (1868 A.D.)

In 787 A.D., The Seventh Ecumenical Council (known as The Second Council of Nicea) decreed, *"We affirm that in Christ there be two wills and two operations according to the reality of each nature, as also taught by the Sixth Synod held at Constantinople, casting out Sergius, Honorius, Cyrus, Pyrrhus, Macarius, and all those who agree with them."*

Popes from the fifth to the eleventh century took an oath prescribed by Gregory II, which included the phrase *"smites with eternal anathema the originators of the new heresy, Sergius,... together with Honorius, because he assisted in the base assertion of heresies."*(*Liber diurnus, ii, 9*)

The Implications

In the past, the Church recognized that a pope could become a formal heretic. Indeed, Honorius did become one, at least, materially.

It could be argued that Honorius was unjustly excommunicated, since the dogma had not yet been defined, and he couldn't be present at the council to explain himself or recant. This would imply that he was only a material heretic (a more accurate phrase would be a Catholic in error), therefore making his excommunication null and void.

The fact is Pope St. Agatho believed that one could be a formal heretic even if the dogma has not been defined. He believed Honorius became a true heretic, which means he also believed a true pope could become a true heretic. This argument is called by some quack apologists to be contrary to Scripture, but obviously the early Church and specifically Pope St. Agatho, did not share this view. It is uncertain what Leo believed about Honorius, although, he did anathematize him for at least allowing heresy.

Be that as it may, Honorius had issued no dogmatic decrees, and only *reigned* for three and a half years after his letter. Therefore, it really is not a matter that needed to be settled and continues unsettled to this day.

Honorius was a true pope and then became a heretic. The anathema charged against him was a decree declaring him to be outside the Body of Christ and therefore not the head of the Body of Christ. If he actually became a formal heretic, he would have immediately lost his pontificate. The declared anathemas are to make public what had already taken place.

St. Francis De Sales (seventeenth century), Doctor of the Church, *The Catholic Controversy,* "*Thus we do not say that the Pope cannot err in his private opinions, as did John XXII; or be altogether a heretic, as perhaps Honorius was. Now when he [the Pope] is explicitly a heretic, he falls ipso facto from his dignity and out of the Church...*"

Notice that St Francis de Sales is not sure if Honorius was a true heretic, but he is sure that when the pope is explicitly a heretic, he loses his office automatically.

Whatever the truth is about Honorius, he is at least a doubtful pope after appearing to have fallen into heresy, which means he might be considered an antipope during that part of his *"pontificate."* Therefore, Honorius should be listed in the *Annuario Pontificio* (official list of popes) because he was a true pope for a time. Whatever the case may be, his condemnation at the Council of Constantinople did not declare or imply that Honorius remained the pope until he died, and the Church has never taken an official stance on it.

Sixth Anomaly:

St. Martin and St. Eugene

Pope St. Martin (reigned 649-654 A.D., died 655 A.D.) was one of the greatest popes who ever lived. He was known for his intellect and great love for the poor. He was also a man of great courage which brought about his cruel and inhumane treatment and death.

He began his pontificate by having himself consecrated apart from the imperial ratification expected from popes in the seventh century. Emperor Constans II rejected St. Martin as the true pope because of his tenacity and independence. He also strongly opposed the monothelite heresy (Christ having only one will) which the emperor professed, so this was strike two against him. St. Martin convened a synod in the Lateran in 649 A.D. strongly condemning the monothelite heresy with twenty canons defining the doctrine of the two wills of Christ. With exceptional fortitude, St. Martin also rejected the powerful emperor's *typus* decree that forbade anyone from speaking about the number of wills of Christ and leveled anathemas at those bishops who sided with the emperor.

The emperor's assassination attempts against St. Martin failed until 653 A.D. when Constans sent the exarch Theodore Calliopas to arrest the bedridden saint, after which he had him declared to be deposed. St. Martin was then sent by ship, which stopped at Naxos, where the saint suffering from gout and dysentery, was made to suffer extreme humiliations.

During his stay, St. Martin wrote letters to the church at Rome expressing and expecting that they not elect another pope while he was still alive.

On his this arrival to Constantinople in 653 A.D., St. Martin would be made to suffer more humiliations and then sent to cruel solitary confinement where he suffered cold, hunger, and thirst. After three months of this treatment, he was found guilty on a bogus charge of treason. He was publically stripped, flogged, chained and dragged through the streets to suffer more humiliations. Emasculated, St. Martin would then be sent into exile by ship, on March 26, 654 A.D. to Chersonesus in the Crimea, where he died in 655 A.D.

Pope St. Martin I in Exile

Eugene was elected pope on August 10, 654 A.D. in St. Martin's place despite his letters of wishes and pleas. However, the good saint relinquished the papacy for the good of the Church.

Pope St. Martin was the last pope to be venerated as a martyr. Eugene would continue to be a courageous pope who would be venerated as another saint.

The Implications

Pope St. Eugene, whose pontificate starts with a bang, was unlawfully elected, but must be considered a true pope since St. Martin abdicated in deference to St. Eugene's status and for the good of the Church.

St. Martin was ignored when asking the Church not to elect another pope. He was one of several popes in history to abdicate from the Chair of Peter. As was the case of one classic example, that of Pope St. Celestine V, who reigned from 1294 to 1296 A.D. His story will be told in the fifteenth anomaly.

Similar to what we've contended about Vigilius' rule over the Catholic Church, St. Eugene's unlawful pontificate should also make him an antipope. He should be considered an antipope before being recognized as the true pope if indeed he was ever a true pope. As in the implications arising from of Vigilius' circumstances, the point here with St. Eugene is that popes need not necessarily be lawfully elected since the Church recognized these two men as true popes.

Because St. Martin's letters were ignored by the allowance of the election of Eugene as pope, it could be argued that the Church at Rome, the See that holds the primacy, went into schism and ceased to be part of the Catholic Church for a time. If this is the case, how did it become reunited with the Church again? It would seem that universal recognition by the rest of the Church is the answer to that question. Thus, the conclusion can be arrived that Rome, in fact, went into schism for a brief time.

If popes can be validly deposed regardless of whether it is lawful or not, then St. Martin's abdication wouldn't matter.

However, there is the matter of the teaching of Pope St. Nicholas I, in his epistle (8), *Proposueramus quidem*, (865 A.D.) to Emperor Michael III on the Immunity and Independence of the Church: "... *"Neither by Augustus, nor by all the clergy, nor by religious, nor by the people will the judge be judged...* **The first seat will not be judged by anyone.**'"

Pope St. Nicholas would continue to explain that his law is the Divine law of God and for good reasons. All spiritual and temporal decisions were to be determined by a pope for the good of the Church and state. However, St. Nicholas was not referring to those crimes of heresy or apostasy, since those crimes have already been judged by God Himself. Once a pope becomes a heretic, he ceases automatically to be pope because God has judged him. The faithful are bound to recognize heretics claiming to be popes and by doing so would not be judging the first seat since the heretic cannot be pope.

Therefore, to depose a true pope for a crime other than heresy or apostasy, would necessarily contradict the teaching of St. Nicholas on the Divine law of God. In other words, for the teaching of Pope St. Nicholas to apply, a pope could not be deposed.

In St. Martin's case, the emperor merely expected the pope to obey him and sign his *typus* decree. St. Martin's refusal to sign and condemnation of it was viewed as a treasonous act. The teaching of Pope St. Nicholas, however, required the emperor to submit to the pope rather than vice-versa. To Peter alone had been given the keys of the kingdom and not to some upstart who lacked them. He simply cannot judge the decision of the pope who not only refused to sign the decree but publically condemned it. The emperor's stance of condemning and deposing the pope was a crime against the Divine law of God and Rome's recognition of St. Martin's deposal and election of Eugene was a schismatic act, plain and simple.

Therefore, St. Martin's deposal was invalid as were all other cases in which popes have been deposed (St. Silverius being another case in point). By electing Eugene, Rome, in fact, temporarily went into schism.

The teaching of St. Nicholas came after the fact and would not be binding retroactively. However, his teaching reflects the Divine law which is binding on the whole world anyway. Whether this was known by Emperor Constans is impossible to tell. If he was ignorant of the law, his action would be a mere sin of ignorance. It's also possible that the emperor simply didn't believe St. Martin was ever a true pope on account of the fact that his consecration was not ratified by him. Thus, the emperor believed that he was deposing an antipope.

If, however, the emperor believed St. Martin was the true pope and knew or suspected the Divine law that no one is to judge the Holy See, his act of deposing the pope must be considered malicious placing all the emperor's adherents in a formal schism.

Seventh Anomaly:

Pope? Stephen II

When Pope Zachary died, the priest named Stephen was elected pope but died four days later on March 752 A.D. He was never consecrated as pope. Canon law at that time required that the consecration was necessary before being recognized as the pope. He was never recognized as a pope by the Church until the sixteenth century, when it became the general opinion that only an election, not the consecration, of a pope is necessary.

Stephen is omitted in *Liber Pontificalis* (The Book of Popes) and is never mentioned again as a pope for another nine hundred years. The *Annuario Pontificio* (official list of popes) included him until 1961 A.D. when Stephen was withheld. Consequently, the numbering to all subsequent popes named Stephen was thrown-off by one.

The Implications

The general opinion that only an election is necessary to cause a candidate to be officially recognized as pope changed over the years. Historically, the universal opinion was that a consecration is necessary. The case of Pelagius I who's never elected but only consecrated would appear to contradict the general opinion that it's the election only, and not the consecration that's required for the Chair of Peter.

If Stephen is truly recognized as a true pope, then the canon laws at that time must be deemed meaningless or understood as being possibly erroneous. The Catholic Church has repeatedly taught that the universal laws of the Church are infallible.

Examples from popes include:

Pope Pius VI, *Auctorem Fidei,* 78 (1794 A.D.) taught that the discipline of the Church cannot be branded as *useless, burdensome, dangerous, or harmful.*

Pope Gregory XVI, *Mirari Vos,* 9 (1832 A.D.): *"Furthermore, the discipline sanctioned by the Church must never be rejected or branded as contrary to certain principles of the natural law. It must never be called crippled, or imperfect or subject to civil authority."*

The same pope taught in *Quo Graviora,* 4-5 (1833 A.D.) that proposition 78 of the constitution *Auctorem fidei* is to be faithfully held by the Church.

Pope Pius XII, *Mystici Corporis,* 66 (1943 A.D.): *"Certainly the loving Mother is spotless in the Sacraments, by which she gives birth to and nourishes her children; in the faith which she has always preserved inviolate; in her sacred laws imposed on all; in the evangelical counsels which she recommends; in those heavenly gifts and extraordinary graces through which, with inexhaustible fecundity, she generates hosts of martyrs, virgins and confessors."*

The theologians:

P. Hermann, *Institutiones Theologiae Dogmaticae,* (4th ed., Rome: Della Pace, 1908), vol. 1, p. 258: *"The Church is infallible in her general discipline. By the term general discipline is understood the laws and practices which belong to the external ordering of the whole Church. Such things would be those which concern either external worship, such as liturgy and rubrics, or the administration of the sacraments. . . . "If she [the Church] were able to prescribe or command or tolerate in her discipline something against faith and morals, or something which tended to the detriment of the Church or to the harm of the faithful, she would turn away from her divine mission, which would be impossible."*

Monsignor G. Van Noort, S.T.D. *Dogmatic Theology,* 2:91 (1958 A.D.): *"The Church's infallibility extends to....ecclesiastical laws passed for the universal Church for the direction of Christian worship and Christian living..."*

Other theologians who taught the infallibility of Church discipline include: A Dorsch, (1928 A.D.), R.M. Schultes, (1931 A.D.), Valentino Zubizarreta, (1948 A.D.), Serapius Iragui, (1959 A.D.) Joachim Salaverri, 1962 A.D.)

Therefore, Stephen must not be considered a true pope or else the infallible teaching of the Church would be rejected.

St. Benedict of Anian (750 – 821 A.D.)
Born about the time of this anomaly, he was the son of Aigulf, Governor of Languedoc. In his early youth, he had the honor of serving, as cup-bearer, King Pepin and his son Charlemagne.

Eighth Anomaly:

Formosus and His Screwy Successors

Formosus was an intelligent man and gifted missionary. However, Pope John VIII exiled him for aspiring to become pope. Pope Marinus I restored him to his office as the bishop of Porto, and he would later be the consecrator of Pope Stephen V in 885 A.D. Upon Stephen's death in 891 A.D., Formosus was raised to the Chair of Peter.

During his pontificate, Formosus had to deal with the tyranny of Emperor Guido and his son and co-Emperor Lambert by petitioning King Arnulf of the East Franks to deliver Rome. After Arnulf was crowned by Formosus, in 896 A.D., he was immediately stuck down with paralysis on his way to conquer Lambert. He fled and abandoned Rome to Lambert, who ruled Rome with a bitter resentment towards Pope Formosus who died shortly after Arnulf's surrender.

After Formosus' death, he was replaced by the short fifteen day reign of Boniface VI who himself had a spurious background. He previously had been defrocked (incurred a deprivation of orders) twice to subdeacon and priest by Pope John VIII for immorality. He was never restored before being elected to the papacy. Two years later, Pope John IX held a synod in Rome declaring the nullity of Boniface's election and prohibiting any such future elections.

Stephen VI was elected after the death of Boniface VI. Springing from his resentment of Formosus for having crowned Arnulf, and his own allegiance to Lambert, Stephen convened a mock trial in January 897 A.D. with the disinterred corpse of Pope Formosus. The macabre trial became known as the 'cadaver synod.'

The rotting corpse was dressed in full regal vestments and propped up on the throne while a deacon terrorized with fear answered with a shaky voice the charges laid against Formosus. Stephen charged Formosus with perjury, violating the canons prohibiting the translation of bishops (occupying the bishopric of Porto and Rome), and coveting the papacy. Stephen declared all the acts of Formosus null and void, including his ordinations. This resulted in the cancellation of Stephen's own consecration as bishop of Anagni. Thus, under canon law, no objections could be raised against his papacy except that he himself was not a bishop. Stephen had the three fingers of Formosus' right hand cut off and his body thrown in the Tiber. It was secretly retrieved by a hermit and buried.

Stephen would continue to make all bishops made by Formosus renounce their Orders as invalid. All these sacrilegious acts of Stephen outraged supporters of Pope Formosus who, in turn, rebelled and deposed Stephen, stripping him of his vestments, and ultimately strangling him to death.

After Stephen's murder in August 897 A.D., Romanus was elected. He was deposed by the people because of his inadequacy in restoring the dignity of Formosus. He died in a monastery as a monk but the date is unknown.

Pope Theodore II, the next pope, restored Formosus, condemned the actions of Stephen, and declared all acts of Formosus valid including those ordinations. (Regardless what any pope declares, all ordinations are valid provided the essential elements of correct minister, form, matter, and intention are present.) Theodore commanded that the body of Formosus be redressed in papal vestments and solemnly buried.

The next pope, John IX, confirmed Theodore's actions and again restored Formosus. John called Formosus' crowning of Arnulf barbaric even though it was forced upon Formosus. He also confirmed the charge against Formosus on the illicit translation of bishops. However, Pope John considered it an exceptional case.

The Implications

The Church was mistaken as to who was the true pope. Even though Boniface VI is listed as a true pope, he should be considered an antipope since Pope John IX declared his election null and void.

There is no question that Stephen's mental capacity was unstable. Because of his insanity, Stephen should be considered an antipope. One theologian says this isn't a novel understanding among canonists:

"Not a few canonists teach that, outside of death and abdication, the pontifical dignity can also be lost by falling into certain insanity, which is legally equivalent to death, as well as through manifest and notorious heresy. In the latter case, a pope would automatically fall from his power, and this indeed without the issuance of any sentence, for the first See (i.e., the See of Peter) is judged by no one ... The reason is that, by falling into heresy, the pope ceases to be a member of the Church. He who is

not a member of a society, obviously, cannot be its head." (*Introductio in Codicem,* 1946 A.D., Udalricus Beste)

Who would not think Stephen was mad after the cadaver synod?

If Romanus did not abdicate due to his deposal, the implication would be that Theodore would actually be an antipope.

Stephen VI's case shows that either the Church has failed to view him as insane, or that She recognized an insane pope given that he is viewed as a true pope by his successors and placed on the official papal list

It seems clear that the Church's acceptance of both Romanus and Stephen being deposed by the faithful and replaced, tells us that the Church believed that a pope could be validly deposed. It is also possible that the Church simply believed that these two lost their office, or were never true popes to begin with. Thus, they were deposing antipopes rather than true popes.

Ninth Anomaly:

John X, Leo VI, and Stephen VII

Pope John X was elected in 911 A.D. because of his accomplished leadership. He successfully fulfilled his role when he built alliances with Italy's leaders to fight against the Muslim invasion. He routed and defeated them in 915 A.D. John would extend his political career with the healing of factions of different sees.

He accomplished several notorious acts as pope. Once, in order to free King Charles III from prison, John made the ridiculous decision to elect the five-year-old son of Count Heribert of Aquitaine to the bishopric of Reims. Emperor Leo VI's fourth marriage would be recognized by John, which made enemies with the Byzantine Patriarch Nicholas I who rejected the marriage. Later, John would make a pact with King Hugh of Italy to secure his position in Rome.

This pope remained independent of the most powerful Roman noble family of Theophylact and Theodora, which happened to be the family whose involvement with the papacy has to go down as one of the most bizarre and twisted. Eldest daughter Marozia had become the force behind this freakish anomaly.

Marozia's power and activity in Rome had been astonishing. She began her career while present at the macabre cadaver synod of Formosus at the age of six. She was the mother of one pope, whom she conceived by another pope, the grandmother of two popes, and yet the great-grandmother of two more popes and, finally, a great-great-grandmother of a final pope. In May of 986 A.D., after hearing her sins and the sins of her grandson *Pope John XII* read to her and then, receiving absolution in prison, Marozia would be beheaded by order of Emperor Otto III, the successor of Charlemagne.

What cost Morozia her head was her interference with the Holy See and the damage it caused. The papacy had become a plaything for the rich and powerful. People lost their lives needlessly.

Suspicious that her power was threatened by Pope John's alliance to the king, Marozia had rallied Roman citizens in revolt against Pope John X and his brother Peter. John's brother was killed right in front of him in the Lateran Palace. The next year, John was deposed by popular demand in May 928 A.D., imprisoned at the Castel Saint'-Angelo, and died there in 929 A.D. He is rumored to have been suffocated with a pillow.

Marozia influenced the election of Leo VI who succeeded John. Leo's short reigned ended with his death seven months later in December 928 A.D. Marozia then secured the election of Stephen VII in December 928 A.D. who replaced Leo while John X was still alive in prison. Almost nothing is known of Stephen's pontificate.

Finally, in 931 A.D., John XI, the illegitimate son of Marozia and Pope Sergius III, would be elected through his powerful mother's influence. He sanctioned her third marriage to King Hugh who was also her brother-in-law, thus breaking Church law. Their tyrannical rule and unlawful marriage incited the people to join forces with Marozia's younger son, Alberic II, who overthrew their rule and had his mother imprisoned. Hugh fled the city with his life. Alberic ruled Italy with an iron fist and also kept Pope John, his half-brother, locked away in the Lateran never to leave.

All four popes are considered true popes on the official papal list.

Marozia and King Hugh from Francisco Bertolini, *Historia de Roma*.

The Implications

We have at least three implications here. First, as we have witnessed in the previous anomalies, the Church believed popes can be deposed by either the people or secular authorities and replaced. In other words, it has not always been the universal belief that popes cannot be deposed.

However, keeping in mind the teaching of Pope Nicholas and the Divine law of God that no one is to judge the Holy See, unless Pope John X consented in giving up the papacy, his disposal would be invalid making Leo and Stephen antipopes with Rome falling into schism once more.

Secondly, Rome can and has fallen from grace and into schism.

Thirdly, the Church can be wrong about who are the true popes. In other words, the Church has mistaken who it is that heads the Church united with Christ.

Papal Family Dynasty Tree

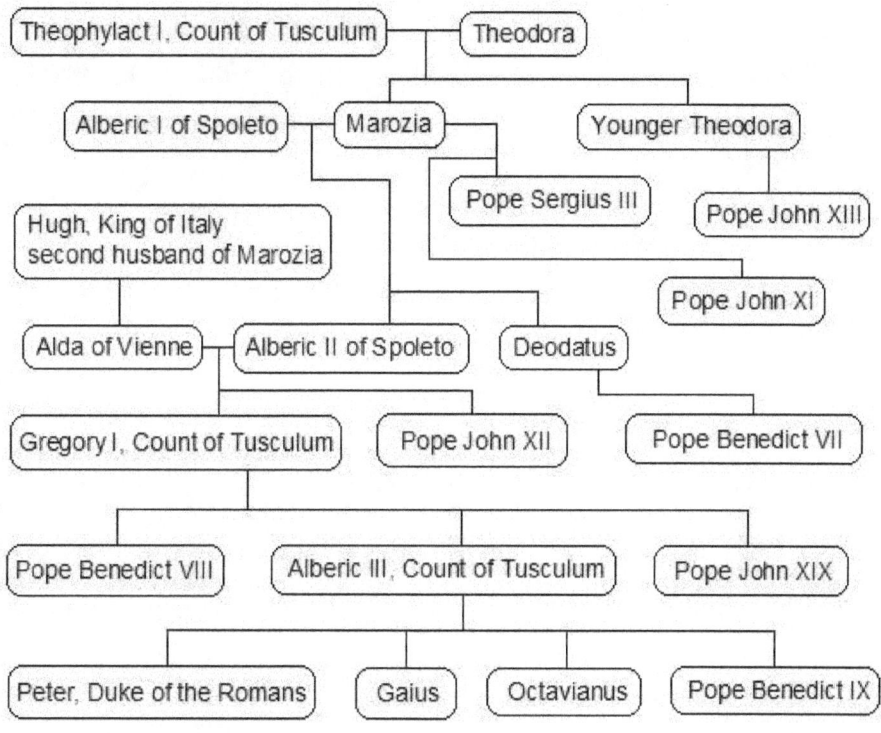

Tenth Anomaly:

John XII, Leo VIII, and Benedict V

Agapetus II was the pope from 946 to 955 A.D. He owed his promotion to Alberic II, prince of Rome. As Alberic lay dying in 954 A.D., he forced the leading Romans, with Pope Agapetus in attendance, to swear a solemn oath on the head of St. Peter the Apostle, that upon the death of Agapetus, they should declare Octavian, (Alberic's bastard son and Morozia's grandson) as the next pope while, at the same time, he would rule as the prince of Rome.

This violated the decree of Pope St. Symmachus (March 1, 499 A.D.) forbidding agreements during a pope's lifetime about the choice of his successor.

Octavian was elected at the age of fifteen and took the name John XII. His life was so filled with debauchery that the Lateran Palace was littered with courtesans and prostitutes. It is recounted that he fornicated with several women, including his father's concubine, Stephana, and his own niece; that he received payments to ordain bishops, one being a ten-year-old; that he blinded his confessor Benedict, cut off the nose, tongue, and two fingers, as well as castrated and killed a cardinal-deacon. Ruthless as any invading barbarian, he wasn't content to stop there, given that he also flayed the skin off Bishop Otger, cut off the hands of Notary Azzo, and beheaded sixty-three of Rome's clergy and nobility. He was also known to do other things contrary to the lifestyle of popes and clerics, such as hunting wildlife and committing arson. He wore battle gear acting like a rogue crusader raping and pillaging his enemies. Most infamously, while partying like a twentieth century frat house, he toasted the devil at the High Altar.

As John was enjoying his debased lifestyle, he ordered the monks of Subiaco Monastery to pray and chant every day one hundred *Kyrie Eleisons* and one hundred *Christe Eleisons* for his soul. The story in Rome was told, however, that the monks prayed instead for his swift death.

Holy Roman Emperor Otto I accepting the surrender of Berengar II of Italy; header reads *Otto I Theutonicorum rex* ("Otto the First, King of the Germans"). *Manuscriptum Medioalense*, (1200 A.D.)

One of John's political acts was crowning Otto I, king of the Germans, as the emperor of the Holy Roman Empire on February 2, 962 A.D. with the agreement that Otto would recognize John as the pope. As Otto rose to power, defeating and imprisoning King Berengar II of Italy, John attempted to have Otto replaced. However, the plan was thwarted and John fled for his life. For John's debauched behavior and perfidy, Otto called and presided over a Roman synod, on December 4. 963 A.D., and deposed John as an apostate and replaced him with Leo VIII.

Leo was an experienced Lateran official but only a layman at the time. He was rushed through the lower orders, and consecrated bishop on December 6. However, unlike the cases with St. Silverius, St. Martin, John X, the teaching of St. Nicholas, etc., that no one can judge the Holy See, was finally, if not woefully late in being recognized by the Church. John instigated a revolt in Rome on January 3, 964 A.D., but Otto, no milquetoast, squashed it with the blood of the insurrectionists.

With the absence of Otto who joined his army, John again retaliated and crushed and tortured the supporters of Leo who, himself, was forced to flee with his life. A synod was called in St. Peter's on February 26, 964 A.D. John deposed and excommunicated Leo as a usurper to the Holy See, for being uncanonically ordained, and for perfidy to his lawful pope. Anyone who was ordained by Leo was forced to confess that his orders were null and void. Haphazardly, John's comeback was fleeting, for Otto returned with a vengeance causing John to take flight and find sanctuary.

Even then, John was the same ole' same ole' in that he hadn't changed. He continued in his licentious ways. On May 14, 964 A.D., while John was indulging in unnatural sexual relations with a Roman matron, *"he was surprised in the act of sin by the matron's angry husband who, in just rage, smashed his skull with a hammer and thus liberated his evil soul into the grasp of Satan...."* The husband would be exonerated for the homicide.

After John's death, the Romans elected Benedict V as successor to John XII. Otto restored Leo to the throne on June 23. Days later, Leo held another synod to depose and degrade Benedict as a usurper to the Holy See. Benedict humbly accepted and died a holy man in 966 A.D. He never tried to regain the papacy after Leo's death in 965 A.D.

John XII, Leo VIII, and Benedict V, are all listed on the official papal list as true popes.

The Implications

The Church has erroneously held an antipope as a true pope. John should be considered an antipope because his election to the papacy violated the decree that forbade such an election. This would mean that Leo was the true pope and Benedict an antipope.

Since John should be considered an antipope, his crowning of Otto I as emperor would be questionable. Although, just as an antipope, if the whole world accepts one as head of state, he would by that fact be head of state regardless.

Second possibility is that the laws of the Church can be ignored without invalidating papal elections. If John was a true pope despite the violated decree and didn't consent in giving up the papacy, then Leo was really an antipope. Benedict would have become the true pope after John. When Benedict abdicated, Leo would have then become pope. If John initially abdicated, Leo would have become the true pope. John would become the antipope after his attempt to retake the papacy back from Leo. Benedict would have then never become pope.

It is all a confusing mess and arguments are made by apologists and historians on behalf of each of these men as true popes. Because of the confusion, it could be argued that all three are doubtful popes at best, which means they were never popes at all.

It's ironic that the Church failed to recognize the Divine law of God as reflected in the teaching of St. Nicholas in the cases of previous popes such as St. Silverius, St. Martin, John X, etc., but did recognize it when it couldn't be applied since John XII was probably an antipope anyway. The conclusion is that the Church either rejected or was ignorant of the Divine law of God. Since the Church in its official capacity cannot reject the Divine laws, it must be concluded that the fault lies in the members of the Church and not necessarily the Church itself.

Today, many Catholics have become disillusioned with the Catholic Church because of its bad priests: Child molesters, sodomites, adulterers, and even bishops moving known sex offenders to other areas without punishment. The fact is the Catholic Church has always had to deal with these kinds of clerics, and as we've seen in this anomaly, those recognized as popes have been as wicked as any priest ever seen in modern society. Our faith is not in popes, bishops, or priests. It is in Christ. The Catholic Church shouldn't be judged on her pathetic members anymore than Christ should be judged on Judas Iscariot.

Eleventh Anomaly:

Benedict VI and Boniface VII

Continuing immediately onward from the last twisted anomaly, things don't get much better when we come to the forthcoming popes. Within a mere ten years of Leo VIII dubious pontificate, Crescentius, the son of Theodora and brother of the previous pope John XIII, incited a revolt against Pope Benedict VI and imprisoned him in Castel Saint'-Angelo in 974 A.D. Not much is known of Benedict except that he confirmed the privileges of monasteries and strictly forbade bishops to charge fees for ordinations and consecrations.

Pope Benedict VI

Despite the fact that Pope Benedict VI was still alive in prison, Cardinal-Deacon Franco was elected and consecrated pope taking the name, Boniface VII. To Boniface's antipathy, the emperor's envoy, Count Sicco, demanded Benedict's release, but Boniface was in no mood to see his pontificate taken from him. He enlisted a priest named Stephen, to do the dirty work of murdering Benedict, doing so by strangulation.

Outraged by Boniface's monstrosity, the people hunted him down with fury. Boniface sought refuge in the Castel Saint'-Angelo until Sicco charged in after him and drove Boniface into the Byzantine territory. No fool, he wasn't going to be left empty-handed. He robbed the papal treasury of the Vatican Basilica as the spoils of ecclesiastical warfare.

When Benedict VII was elected and consecrated pope in 974 A.D., one of his first acts was to hold a synod to excommunicate Boniface VII. But Boniface had more tricks of his sleeves. He somehow re-established himself as Supreme Pontiff, until a year later when Emperor Otto II drove him out again in 981 A.D. Benedict would die within two more years.

During those days, therefore, the Chair of Peter was vacant for five months. Similarly to how Justinian forced Pelagius to occupy the Chair of Peter four hundred and thirty years earlier, Otto did his own forcing by making Peter Canepanova accept being made the Roman Pontiff taking John XIV as his papal name. This took place in December 983 A.D. and was a source of consternation to the Romans. Otto was John's only ally against the angry mob that sought his removal but he died with malaria days after John's coronation.

Otto's death left poor John as easy pickings when Boniface returned, yet again, to claim the papacy. Armed with funds from Byzantium and the money he had stolen from Rome, he bought off powerful leaders to help him. Defenseless, Pope John XIV was seized, brutally assaulted, and imprisoned in the Castel Saint'-

Angelo in 984 A.D. Four months later and nearly dead by starvation, by order of Boniface, Pope John XIV was sent to his eternal reward via poisoning.

It appears that Boniface was assassinated in 985 A.D. The outraged Romans stripped Boniface's corpse of his papal vestments and utterly desecrated it. Naked, it was dragged through the streets in front of the statue of Marcus Aurelius in the Lateran, and on the Capitol, where a virtual feeding frenzy then took place. People from all over rushed to the corpse spitting and trampling it. Not satisfied with this carnage, the indignant crowd stabbed the mangled corpse with their spears.

Henceforth, Boniface became known as *"malefatius"*. He was considered a valid pope for a short period after the death of John XIV, Even being placed on the official list of popes. By the twentieth century, however, he fell from grace, being removed from this list in 1904 A.D.

The Implication

Boniface's removal from the list just over a century ago shows the Church's recognition of his illegitimacy. The implication is that an antipope had been viewed wrongly by the Catholic Church for more than a millennium.

Twelfth Anomaly:

The Hodgepodge of Popes Benedict IX, Sylvester III, Gregory VI, Clement II, Damasus II, and St. Leo IX

If the last two anomalies didn't leave you jolted, then perhaps the next freakish aberration will.

After Pope Sylvester II was murdered in 1003 A.D., his successor, Pope John XVII, was poisoned seven months later. In less than ten years, Antipope Gregory and Pope Benedict VIII would duke it out. After Benedict's death, his brother Romanus seized the Chair of Peter, calling himself John XIX. When he died under suspicious circumstances in 1033 A.D., things would get even crazier and downright creepy.

The head of the ruling family, Alberic III, took his own twelve-year-old son, Theophylact, who also was the nephew of both John XIX and Benedict VIII, had papal clothes made to fit the young lad, and lifted him onto the papal throne. He was consecrated pope in 1032 A.D., taking the name, Benedict IX.

This event is so unbelievable that later sources would say that Benedict was really in his twenties. However, if we consider that the five-year-old son of Count Heribert of Aquitaine was raised to the bishopric of Reims by Pope John X, there is no reason to disbelieve that the most powerful man in the region could have his twelve-year-old son recognized as pope. This is just how things were done in what could be rightly called *"dark ages."*

Benedict was a veritable monster. A bisexual who dabbled in the occult, he led a violent and dissolute life, sodomizing animals and ordering murders. *"Feasting on immorality"* and *"a demon from hell"* is how St. Peter Damiani described him. Pope

Victor III told how he raped, murdered, and did other kinds of unspeakable things. In his third book of Dialogues, Victor wrote, *"His life as a pope was so vile, foul, and execrable, that I shudder to think of it."*

Within less than a year, a plot to have him strangled went awry, Benedict escaping unharmed. Fed-up with his rank unholiness, the Romans drove him out in 1044 A.D., and elected John of Sabina as Pope Sylvester III, perhaps through bribery. The powerful family of Tusculum, however, again put Benedict back on the throne, and Sylvester had to flee.

In two months, Benedict found a buyer to the throne. His godfather, John Gratian, made the agreement that when John became pope, Benedict would receive for the rest of his life the entire tribute of the English Church. The documented arrangement was called *Peter's Pence*. John took the name Gregory VI in 1045 A.D., and Benedict remained in the Lateran Palace as a gigolo, turning the place into the best brothel in Rome. At the same time, Sylvester was staying at St. Mary Major's attempting to be recognized as the true pope. Benedict, unsatisfied with being the second notch on the totem pole, tried to depose Gregory.

In September 1046 A.D., Holy Roman Emperor Henry III came to town prepared to make things right. He called the Council of Sutri, expelled the three *"popes"* and elected his own pope. The German Clement II was the next to be handed the keys of the kingdom. No slouch, this reformer took to the stage and condemned simony in another synod. He decreed forty days of hard penance for anyone who knowingly got ordained by simoniac bishops. However, Benedict would have none of it. He had Clement killed by poisoning and climbed back onto the papal throne for another eight months until Emperor Henry returned and took charge of events. Benedict had to flee as Henry mounted another German onto the throne. Poppo of Brixin took the name Damasus II on July, 17, 1048 A.D. He died twenty-three days later and amazingly perhaps, Benedict resumed where he left off...at the top. Henry was determined to see Benedict expelled from out of the picture for good. He deposed Benedict for the last time and had Pope St. Leo IX succeed Damasus in February 1049 A.D.

Pope St. Leo IX

St. Leo wasted no time in convening the synod in the Lateran condemning simony and clerical unchastity. Benedict was charged with simony and then excommunicated for not appearing. St. Leo reinstituted Clement's rule of penance and deposed many simoniac bishops. He even reordained men who were initially ordained by simoniac bishops. This means that simoniac bishops were not recognized as valid bishops or their consecrations were considered doubtful or invalid (see pp. 137-138). Benedict continued to think of himself as the rightful pope.

It is said that St. Leo, on his death bed, lifted the excommunication of Benedict IX, prayed that one day he would see the truth, and change his life. Leo died in 1053 A.D. and was succeeded by Victor II on April 13, 1055 A.D.

Benedict IX was still alive when Victor was pope. There is a neat bedtime story told by an abbot from the Abbey of Grottaferrata shortly after Benedict's death (late in 1055 or early 1066 A.D.) that Benedict received the grace of Leo's prayer and converted.

With the possible exception of Sylvester, all these men were considered true popes and have continued as such on the Church's official list.

The Implications

The Church believed that a child could be pope. Benedict was considered a true pope even at the age of twelve. If Benedict's abdication were valid then Gregory would have been a legit pope. If Gregory was legit and accepted being deposed, then Clement was legit. If Benedict's abdication was invalid, then Gregory, Clement, Damasus, and Victor were antipopes. Leo would have started off as an antipope and later becoming a true pope.

If Benedict were a continued Satanist, then he would have ipso facto not been a true pope. This would make Sylvester the true pope until he died in 1063 A.D., unless he accepted being deposed. This would make all subsequent *popes* antipopes.

If simony invalidated an election as it surely did within the next few years under Pope Nicholas II (see the nineteenth anomaly chapter), then Benedict became an antipope, as did Gregory. Sylvester would have been a doubtful pope for his possible bribery. Clement would have been the true pope as were those that followed him.

There is enough confusion here to render them all doubtful until Clement.

St. Leo's lifting of the excommunication of Benedict was for not showing up at the synod, thus rendering him schismatic for disobedience.

The implications from this historic anomaly are that the Church can't tell for sure who were the true popes, and making its official papal list incorrect again. It also tells us that the Church doesn't seem to care whether these men were ever true popes since an explanation has never been given. It just doesn't matter.

As a side note: Pope Martin V, at the Council of Constance, Session VIII, (May 4, 1415 A.D.) condemned the errors of John Wycliffe for teaching that a pope cannot be evil and a member of the devil. During Session XV (July 6, 1415 A.D.) of the same council, Pope Martin also condemned John Hus for teaching practically the same thing as Wycliffe.

These condemnations would not have applied to Benedict IX who did more than merely belong to the devil. All men in mortal sin belong to the devil, and surely many popes have been in mortal sin. Innocent III was presented as one example in the introduction of this book. Satanism is a religion and a Satanist would not be a Catholic. Therefore, a Satanist could not be the Roman Pontiff.

John Hus at the Council of Constance 1415 A.D. by Václav Brožík (1851–1901 A.D.)

Thirteenth Anomaly:

Antipope Benedict X

John Mincius, Cardinal-Bishop of Velletri, was coercively elected as Pope Benedict X. Cardinal-Bishop of Ostia, St. Peter Damiani, whose job it was to consecrate pope-elects, altogether opposed Benedict X because the Roman clerics made an oath to the previous Pope Stephen IX not to elect a new pope until his confidant, Hildebrand could be present. Hildebrand was absent because he was off spreading the Gospel in Germany at the time.

When the Second Lateran Council affirmed the validity of Holy Orders of simoniacs, St. Peter Damiani (above, 1007 – 1072 A.D.) was proven to have known more than Pope St. Leo IX. (See p. 138)

Benedict functioned as the pope for nine months until the opposing cardinals elected Pope Nicholas II at Siena in December 1058 A.D. In January 1059 A.D., the new pope held a synod at Sutri and excommunicated Benedict X as a usurper to the papal throne, and for disregarding the oath he made to Pope Stephen.

Benedict took sanctuary in Gerard's castle at Galeria. After being ransacked in 1059 A.D., Benedict relinquished his papal insignia, and abnegated all claim to the papacy. A month later, Hildebrand imprisoned him. Not satisfied with this decision, Hildebrand deposed, degraded, and placed Benedict on house arrest. When Hildebrand finally ascended to the throne as Pope Gregory VII, he forgave Benedict and provided him with a Catholic burial.

The Implications

In an unhappy gestation period of sorts, the Church mistakenly acknowledged an antipope as a true pope for nine months.

During the trial conducted by Hildebrand, Benedict confessed that his election was invalid when he pleaded with Hildebrand that he was forced onto the throne and without proper procedures. Therefore, it could not be argued that he was ever a true pope.

Fourteenth Anomaly:

Anacletus II vs. Innocent II

Following the death of Pope Callistus II in December 1124 A.D., a tumultuous election ensued. Two powerful families were at odds with cardinals accompanying each side. Cardinal-Priest Teobalbo was proclaimed Celestine II by the majority of cardinals along with the Peirleoni family. During the installation ceremony, the rival Frangipani family, led by Robert with the help of armed troops supplied by Chancellor Haymaric, burst in and hijacked the ceremony. Sword in hand, Robert fiercely announced Cardinal Lamberto of Ostia as the next pope. Militarily deposed, Celestine stepped down never to be consecrated, and Lamberto was enthroned as Pope Honorius II. The pope's adversaries would have to wait for the next election if they were to regain the papacy.

Six years later, Honorius fell ill. Aware of the menacing Peirleoni's and the mercenary populace wanting a sympathetic pope of their cause in the next election, Chancellor Haymaric moved the pope to the monastery of San Gregorio on the Caelian as the Frangipani family kept a stronghold over the monastery. When Honorius' died in the middle of the night on February 14, 1130 A.D., Haymaric provided a secret burial in the monastery and proceeded once again to protect the papacy with a covert election. Backed by the Corsi and Frangipani families, sixteen members of the Sacred College, including the cardinal-bishop of Ostia, enthroned Cardinal-Deacon of San Angelo, Gregorio Papareschi, as Pope Innocent II. This group would be later called the *squadronisti*.

Three hours later, outraged by the *coup d'état*, the majority of the other cardinals, backed by the Pierleoni family, elected Cardinal Peitro of Sta Maria of Trastevere as pope. He was enthroned by the bishop of Porto, the dean of the Sacred College, taking the name, Anacletus II. Both were consecrated on the same day, February 23rd.

Nearly all of Rome rallied around him. Fearing the opposition, the Frangipani family deserted Pope Innocent II and joined Anacletus II. When Innocent took flight into France, his greatest champion, St. Bernard of Clairvaux, convinced the whole world to join him. St. Bernard won over King Louis VI of France, King Henry I of England, and King Lothair III of Germany.

St. Bernard of Clairvaux, Cathedral Treasury, Troyes.
On his own authority, St. Bernard rejected the papal claimant recognized by Rome as the true pope.

When St. Bernard wrote letters to bishops on why Innocent should be recognized over Anacletus, they listened. As he gathered steam for Innocent's cause, Anacletus ruled as pope and amassing wealth in the process. On Christmas day, 1130 A.D., he appointed Duke Roger II the first king of Sicily and Calabria. Attempting his own turn-around, Anacletus sent out letters to the kings of France and Germany and all the leading clerics, but to no avail. St. Bernard had won. Two great synods were held at Reims and Piacenza proclaiming Innocent as the legitimate pope and anathematizing Anacletus.

King Lothair conducted Innocent to Rome in the spring of 1133 A.D., but Anacletus safely barricaded himself within the walls of Castel Saint'-Angelo. Because the Anacletans successfully secured St. Peter's, Pope Innocent crowned King Lothair, Holy Roman Emperor, in the Lateran. However, upon Lothair's departure, Anacletus drove out Innocent who fled to Pisa. Anacletus ruled peacefully as the Supreme Pontiff, albeit, invalidly until 1137 A.D. when Emperor Lothair returned, but he suddenly died in December. Anacletus died the following month in January 1138 A.D. Victor IV was elected in place of the antipope Anacletus, but St. Bernard wasn't finished. He effectively converted Victor, who in turn, submitted to Innocent thus ending the schism.

The Implications

The majority doesn't always get it right. In this case, the minority won the day. Even though virtually all of Rome accepted Anacletus, very few rejected him, and one man stood against him persuading the world to do the same. St. Bernard would get help from St. Norbert of Xanten, and together they influenced the world to reject the Catholic authorities which consisted of the majority of cardinals, including the bishop of Porto.

St. Bernard of Clairvaux on his own authority judged whom the world believed to be the pope as an antipope. Thus, faithful Catholics are bound to judge and reject false *"popes"* as antipopes. This power of the Catholic laymen to do so comes from Christ's warning to beware of wolves in sheep's clothing in the Gospel of Matthew 7:15.

In the twentieth century, good and faithful Catholics on their own authority will judge as antipopes whom the majority of the world believes to be true popes. The argument that mere men cannot judge popes will be used over and over. Point in fact, mere men cannot judge true popes as antipopes but they can judge antipopes to be antipopes. Therefore, the argument used against the faithful Catholic is a false and misleading accusation.

If the antipope is a heretic/apostate, as the current claimant to the papal throne, then the faithful must reject him regardless. The current law of the Catholic Church confirms this simple statement as it reflects the Divine law of God.

All the popes and saints, who taught on the subject, confirmed the Divine law that a pope cannot be a heretic, apostate, or schismatic.

At times, Canon 2232 of the 1917 Code of Canon Law of the Catholic Church will be used by quack apologists to defend heretics/apostates/schismatics as those who should be recognized as members of the Church under certain circumstances. However, the law makers never had in mind when devising the law the specific crimes of heresy, apostasy, etc. because these entail an automatic excommunication under all circumstances.

Heretics, apostates, etc. are not Catholics and therefore should not be assumed as Catholics with the ability to hold ecclesiastical offices, such as the papacy. Imagine a non-Catholic as the head of the Catholic Church under any circumstance. It's quite ridiculous. In the past, many popes have clearly taught that heretics, etc are not members of the Church. A few such examples:

Pope Innocent III, *Eius exemplo*, December 18, 1208 A.D.: *"By the heart we believe and by the mouth we confess the one Church, not of heretics, but the Holy Roman, Catholic, and Apostolic Church."*

Pope Eugene IV, Council of Florence, *Cantate Domino*, 1441 A.D.: *"The Holy Roman Church firmly believes, professes and preaches that all those who are outside the Catholic Church, not only pagans but also Jews or heretics and schismatics, cannot share in eternal life and will go into the everlasting fire which was prepared for the devil and his angels, unless they are joined to the Church before the end of their lives."*

Pope Leo XIII, *Satis Cognitum* (# 9), June 29, 1896 A.D.: *"The practice of the Church has always been the same, as is shown by the unanimous teaching of the Fathers, who were wont to hold as outside Catholic communion, and alien to the Church, whoever would recede in the least degree from any point of doctrine proposed by her authoritative Magisterium."*

Pope Pius XII, *Mystici Corporis Christi* (# 23), June 29, 1943 A.D.: *"For not every sin, however grave it may be, is such as of its own nature to sever a man from the Body of the Church, as does schism or heresy or apostasy."*

The same quacks that use canon 2232 against Catholics insist that a declaration is needed to oust an antipope from the papacy. This is illogical. If all the authorities adhere to the same heresies as the antipope in question, then a declaration will never come. This would undoubtedly lock one up in heresy and schism since he can't get out of the mess. Besides, an antipope doesn't possess the papacy and there is nothing to oust him from, except the Lateran where he may be living.

The faithful are to recognize what God has already done and declare an antipope as an antipope and reject everything that is connected to such a person. The modern pseudo-Catholics that continue to condemn devout Catholics for rejecting the current papal claimant on the basis that no one can judge him, would have also condemned St. Bernard of Clairvaux, St. Norbert of Xanten, and many others for doing precisely the same thing. Those pseudo-Catholics would have followed the antipopes of history just as they follow the one now, and for the same reason.

Fifteenth Anomaly:

The Long Interregnums of the Thirteenth and Fourteenth Centuries

(The following anomaly is actually a series of anomalies lumped together to illustrate the same point.)

As usual, there were serious factions within the Church and nowhere was this more evident than in the High Middle Ages. When Pope Clement IV died on November 29, 1268 A.D., the French and Italian cardinals were at odds with each other over territorial powers. The law at the time was the two-thirds majority vote, and neither side was giving in to the other. Almost two years passed and the Romans were becoming indignant over the delay. They had already been patient enduring twenty-five years of long exasperating interregnums, so the well of patience dried up.

Disputes erupted when Pope Gregory IX became mortal enemies with German Emperor Fredrick II. Gregory excommunicated Fredrick when he returned the deed by imprisoning two out of the twelve cardinals in existence. By time Pope Gregory IX died on August 21, 1241 A.D., at the ripe old age of one hundred, Europe was in shambles. Rioting and murder filled the streets of Rome. Businesses collapsed and sanitation was deplorable. To stabilize the situation, the governor of Rome, Senator Matteo Rosso Orsini, stepped in and enforced the Church to elect a new pope.

He began by humbling the ten cardinals with humiliations such as tying them up like cattle, one hand to one foot, and then beating, mocking and cursing them in the town square. Orsini made it clear to the cardinals that he wasn't fooling around. The next step taken by Orsini was locking them up in the main hall of the Septizodium to elect a pope and voilà, the papal conclave was born. Guards were posted all around the hall, killing anyone on site who attempted to enter or leave the building.

A fragment of the Septizonium, engraving dates to 1582 A.D.

Still in amidst of summertime, the hot and humid conditions were unbearable and the cardinals' living conditions were horrid. They never changed their clothes and had to exist in a stinking dungeon-like room, filled with their left-over urine and feces and those of the guards who couldn't leave their posts.

Despite the trying conditions, the stubborn cardinals remained divided. One side was trying to appease Frederick by electing a sympathetic pope, and the other side wanted a pope who would side with Frederick's enemies to make war against him. In an attempt to be freed from their prison, the cardinals elected Cardinal Humberto Romano who would immediately abdicate. Orsini, not fooled by their trick, commanded them to elect someone else, or he would dig up Pope Gregory, and throw his decayed remains in the room while they decided. If this didn't persuade them to speed up the process, Orsini threatened he'd simply kill them all. Locked up for fifty-five days in a single room and scared for their lives, they finally elected Pope Celestine IV who died two weeks later, never to be consecrated. The frightened cardinals took flight to their palaces and fortresses, not wanting to endure another conclave.

Emperor Frederick wanted his sympathetic pope. He released Cardinal Oddo Colonna and Cardinal Jacopo of Praeneste from their prison in Capua and ordered the eleven cardinals to elect a new pope. They boondoggled and Fredrick destroyed their properties which left Rome in desperation for repair. The eighteen month interregnum ended in 1243 A.D. with the election of Pope Innocent IV. The next two papal elections went without a hitch.

However, when Pope Clement IV died, the eighteen cardinal college was again divided when they met in the town of Viterbo. These narcissistic cardinals were rich and powerful who lorded their power over the rest of society. Their division grew from each of them wanting to rule the nations and from vying for whom among them would be pope and ruler of them all. They actually agreed on electing Philippo Beniti, head of the Order of Servites, but Philippo refused, knowing that his life was at a great risk.

By March of 1271 A.D., the rulers of the surrounding areas began to arrive in Viterbo trying to persuade the cardinals to come in agreement. The city was falling apart. Two armies occupied the city and dead bodies were strewn throughout. The countryside was more dangerous than *"walking among the Muslims of Africa,"* as the saying went. During Holy Mass, attended by all the cardinals and clerics, viceroy of Tuscany, Guido, marched right up behind Prince Henry of Cornwall as he was in line to receive the

Holy Eucharist, and stabbed Henry eleven times with his dagger flinging blood on nearby spectators. Guido dragged the prince by the hair and flung him outside the church. The bickering prideful cardinals became more angry and divided over the incident and things looked pretty hopeless. Apparently, the cardinals had short memories of the not so distant past.

The Church was now without a pope for over two and half years. The resultant long-suffering Italians had had enough. They weren't going to stand any longer for this prolonged popelessness.

As Orsini did decades ago, the governor of Viterbo, Albert de Montbuono with captain of the Viterban militia, Ramiro Galli, locked the cardinals up in the papal palace. The cardinals were only allowed bread and water for sustenance. When the cardinals procrastinated, the Viterbans removed the roof exposing them to the elements of heat, cold, and rain. Cardinal John of Toledo remarked, *"Sure! They had to take off the roof. How else could the Holy Ghost enter among us?"*

The hard-headed cardinals threatened excommunication to the Viterbans if the roof wasn't put back on, locks removed, and a better supply and selection of food. However, the powerful Savelli family claimed to be the *"Custodians of the Conclave"* and threaten to kill anyone who gave in to the cardinals' wishes. The governor, magistrates, captain, and townspeople told the cardinals, *"We may live excommunicated and without religious worship. But your Eminences will surely die of hunger, disease, and hardship. Choose a pope!"*

Months passed, the cardinals remained obstinate. On September 1, 1271 A.D., it took a fiery sermon from St. Bonaventure to shame the cardinals into submission. They elected six compromisers who that evening chose the sixty-one-year-old non-cardinal, Teobaldo Visconti. On November 19, 1271 A.D., he was homeward bound from a pilgrimage to the Holy Land when the news arrived of his election. He was welcomed home at Viterbo on February 12, 1272 A.D. and took the name Gregory X. His consecration and coronation took place on March 27, 1272 A.D., three years and four months after Clement IV's death.

The thirteenth century on into the fourteenth, long interregnums became almost routine. Hadrian V undid the strict conclave rules ordered by Gregory X and therefore, after the death of Pope John XXI on May 20, 1277 A.D., six months passed before seven cardinals chose Cardinal Giovanni Gaetano of the Orsini family as Pope Nicholas III. When Nicholas died on August 22, 1280 A.D., the cardinals argued another six months before being pressured by King Charles of Sicily to elect Pope Martin IV. It took eleven months after the death of Pope Honorius IV on April 3, 1287 A.D., for the cardinals, six of whom died from the summer heat, to elect Pope Nicholas IV February 22, 1288 A.D.

When Pope Nicholas IV died April 4, 1292 A.D., twelve cardinals, divided as always, debated twenty-seven months before electing Peter Murrone as Pope St. Celestine V July 5, 1294 A.D. Although, St. Celestine reestablished Pope Gregory X's conclave rules, he didn't want to live life as the pope. On December 13, 1294 A.D., Celestine resigned from the papacy returning to a life as Peter, the poor, barefoot monk. The Romans were flabbergasted. Gaetani would take over the throne as Boniface XIII. To eradicate all potential opposition to his reign, Boniface caught, imprisoned and executed St. Peter Murrone on May 19, 1296 A.D., even though Peter had no intention of making a comeback.

Seven years later, Blessed Pope Benedict XI would leave Rome where his life was in danger. On July 7, 1304 A.D., in Perugia where he settled, Benedict was assassinated with a plate of poisoned figs. Apparently, the re-enacted conclave rules meant little in shortening interregnums for eleven months passed before the divided cardinals elected Betrand de Got June 5, 1305 A.D. He was crowned in Lyons, France as Pope Clement V.

He settled in Avignon, France, never to reign in the city of Peter and Paul, thus inaugurating the seventy-two-year hiatus from Rome. This first Avignon line of popes, an anomaly itself, was labeled *"The Babylon captivity of the papacy"* because the Italian poet Petrarch wrote that Avignon had become, *"home to wine, women, song, and priests who cavorted as if all their glory consisted not in Christ but in feasting and unchastity."* Dante wrote a letter to Clement chastising him, *"You have neglected to guide the Chariot of the Bride of the Crucified along the path so clearly marked for Her."* Later came the illustrious St. Catherine of Sienna's famous petrine rebuke, *"At the Papal Court which ought to have been a paradise of virtue, my nostrils were assailed by the odors of hell."*

Pope Celestine V returning to his life as Peter Murrone.

When Clement died April 20, 1314 A.D., the twenty-three cardinals, five of whom were Clement's relatives because of nepotism, and King Philip V of France who arranged the conclave, resolved the interregnum after two years by electing the bishop of Porto, Jacques Duèse on August 7, 1316 A.D. He was crowned September 5, 1316 A.D. as Pope John XXII.

The Implications

Just as we've seen in the first anomaly, the Roman Catholic Church continued unified in faith and remained the visible Body of Christ despite being without a pope during those long interregnums. The law of perpetual succession remains with the absence of a pope. As always, Christ is the Head of the Church during interregnum periods. The Church is never a headless monster.

The governor of Rome, Senator Matteo Rosso Orsini threatened to kill all the cardinals if they didn't elect a pope. The townspeople Viterbo under its governor also threatened the lives of the cardinals during their conclave, thus revealing that they knew that a pope could be installed without cardinals under extraordinary conditions, despite the law at that time that a vote of two-thirds majority of the cardinals was required.

The First Vatican Canon stated: *"if anyone then says that it is not from the institution of Christ the Lord Himself, or by Divine right that the blessed Peter has perpetual successors in the primacy over the universal Church . . . let him be anathema."*

Cardinal Billot explains, *"When it would be necessary to proceed with the election, if it is impossible to follow the regulations of papal law, as was the case during the Great Western Schism, one can accept, without difficulty, that the power of election could be transferred to a General Council...Because natural law prescribes that, in such cases, the power of a superior is passed to the immediate inferior because this is absolutely necessary for the survival of the society and to avoid the tribulations of extreme need."(De Ecclesia Christi)*

No Church law or the inability to follow the law under normal circumstances can impede or prohibit the Divine right that Peter has perpetual successors. The Church throughout the ages has instinctively understood this dogma, especially in light of the anomalies of the thirteenth and fourteenth centuries.

Map of Italy

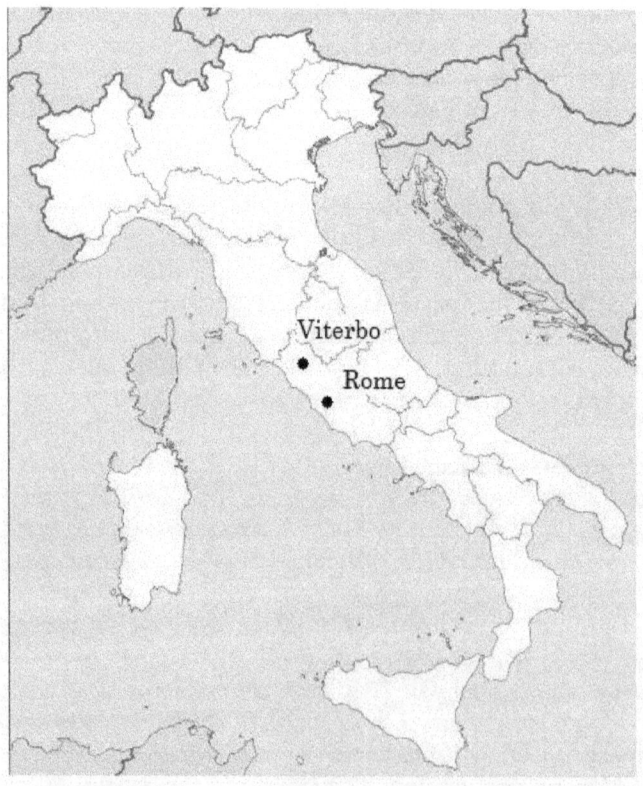

Sixteenth Anomaly

Pope? Hadrian V

Dante's 'The souls of the avaricious: Hadrian V in Purgatory' by Gustave Doré

The fiery Blessed Pope Gregory X would institutionalize the conclave with stiff rules and regulations. After the death of his successor, Blessed Pope Innocent V, the second Vatican approved conclave took place. Through the influence of King Charles of Anjou, Ottobono Fieschi was elected in the Lateran on July 11, 1276 A.D., taking the name, Hadrian V (also known as Adrian V).

He was made a cardinal-deacon by his uncle Pope Innocent IV. Hadrian suspended Gregory's rules on the conclave and planned as *pope* to moderate them. However, taking a leave of absence from Rome due to the hot weather, he died on August 18, 1276 A.D. never to be ordained, consecrated, or crowned.

While Dante, in his *Divine Comedy*, placed Hadrian in purgatory for the sin of avarice, the Church placed him on the official list of popes.

The Implications

We have a contradiction with the *Annuario Pontificio* (official list of popes). Stephen II was withheld from the list for not being a consecrated bishop, yet Hadrian is given the benefit of the doubt even though he is in the same boat as Stephen. So which is it?

We know that a layman can become the pope, but can a pope be a layman? There are conflicting views on this point.

In an address to the Second World Congress of the Lay Apostolate on October 5, 1957 A.D., Pope Pius XII taught, *"Even if a layman were elected pope, he could accept the election only if he were fit for ordination and willing to be ordained but the power to teach and govern, as well as the divine gift of infallibility, would be granted to him from the very moment of his acceptance, even before his ordination."*

Historically, the Church has not always recognized unconsecrated popes. Stephen II was not, and Leo VIII was rushed through the lower orders so that his consecration as bishop would qualify him as pope. However, on this point in history with Hadrian V, the faithful appears to accept a layman pope, since Hadrian's suspension of Pope Gregory's conclave laws was recognized.

It has been a general opinion of theologians that one becomes pope immediately upon election regardless whether consecrated or not. General opinions are doctrines that belong in the realm of free opinions not binding on the faithful. It is true that the majority of theologians, if not all, agree with this teaching of Pope Pius XII. However, his teaching is not binding on the faithful because it does not fall under the rubric of extraordinary magisterial teaching nor does it fall under universal and ordinary teaching. It is simply an address to a group of people where Pope Pius XII gives his own opinion which could, quite conceivably, be heretical.

The fact remains that the Church in different periods of history has differed on whether popes must be consecrated bishops.

Seventeenth Anomaly:

The Mistaken John XXII

Pope John XXII

We have seen from the fifteenth anomaly how it took two years for the cardinals to decide that the bishop of Porto, Jacques Duèse should be the Roman Pontiff, but the anomaly doesn't stop there. John XXII was the second Avignon pope before the Great Schism who cemented the papacy in France. He inherited a bankrupt church with corrupt clergy, and although old and feeble, he wasted no time in reforming the Church both spiritually and financially.

At the same time, he attempted to resolve the two factions within the Franciscan order known as the Spirituals and the Conventuals. At one point in 1317 A.D., he reprimanded the Spirituals in the bull *Quorumdam exigit*. Those that remained obstinate were captured by the Inquisition and four of them were burned at the stake. When the fanatical Spirituals declared the absolute poverty of Christ and the Apostles, Pope John denounced the heresy on November 12, 1323 A.D. in *Quum inter nonnullos.* He subsequently took away the groups own property, the titularly vested in the Holy See.

The angry Spirituals led by Michael of Cesena branded Pope John as a heretic and the antichrist and the Roman Church as the *"Whore of Babylon."* By 1325 A.D., the majority affirmed their loyalty to Pope John by deposing Michael while he led a large minority into schism. Pope John summoned Michael to Avignon, but in 1328 A.D. the general fled with William of Ockman to the court of King Louis of Bavaria who was excommunicated in 1324 A.D. after defeating Fredrick I of Austria and denouncing the teaching found in *Quum inter nonnullos.*

After Louis entered triumphantly into Rome and elected antipope Nicholas V in 1328 A.D., the Romans reacted violently and Louis retreated and Nicholas bowed out and sought forgiveness from Pope John who eventually pardoned him. However, Louis and the Spirituals, continued enemies on John, endeavored to avenge the Avignon pope. They thought they found their chance when on All Saints Day 1331 A.D. Pope John contradicted a universally held Catholic doctrine by stating in a sermon that souls do not attain the Beatific Vision until after the General Judgment. The schismatics exploited the incident and urged the cardinals to condemn the pope as a heretic.

In November 1333 A.D., Pope John wrote to King Phillip IV that there was no dogma and that Catholics were free to disagree on the matter. The next month at the University of Paris, church authorities pointedly determined that Pope John's teaching was merely his personal opinion but in error nonetheless. On January 3, 1334 A.D., Pope John declared that he had not intended to contradict the Faith. Later that same year, while on his deathbed, John retracted his heresy and affirmed what his successor, Benedict XII would assert in the Constitution

"Benedictus Deus" (1336 A.D.) that the blessed souls of the dead *"see the face of the triune God immediately after death."*

The Implications

Since the doctrine was not defined until after the death of the pope, John should be considered a good-will Catholic in error and not a heretic.

Quack apologists of Vatican II use the argument against Catholic *sedevacantists* that Pope John XXII's teaching was manifestly heretical and yet remained the pope. Therefore, heresies taught by Roncalli (John XXIII) through Ratzinger (Benedict XVI) would not cause them to lose their pontificates. However, as we have seen, the Avignon pope's mere sermon did not contradict any defined teaching, unlike those of John XXIII through Benedict XVI, some of which were formal (Vatican II). See the twentieth anomaly chapter.

Eighteenth Anomaly:

The Great Schism

The era of the late fourteenth century was a mess of unprecedented measure. Popes Urban VI, Boniface IX, Innocent VII, Gregory XII, Clement VII, Benedict XIII, Clement VIII are all highly disputed.

Thirty years after the Hundred Years War began, in the spring of 1367 A.D., Pope Urban V left Avignon for Viterbo and on to Rome only to return to France in the late summer of 1370 A.D. after his four year stint in Italy. Europe was unsettled by the act and Pope Gregory XI returned the papacy to Rome on January 17, 1377 A.D. When Gregory was on his deathbed, he knew the cardinals and the faithful would be divided because of national pride and urged the whole Church to accept whoever was elected. He left six French cardinals in France barring them from the next conclave to appease the anxious Italians.

When Pope Gregory died, a rioting crowd, fearing the election of a Frenchman and returning the papacy to Avignon, pressured the fifteen of the sixteen cardinals to elect an Italian to keep the peace. When they chose Pope Urban VI (Bartolomeo Prignano) on April 8, 1378 A.D., the shocked pope-elect was bombarded by the rioters intensifying the moment to the point that Prignano doesn't consent to his election as he tells the people that it is was all a hoax. The cardinals fled with their lives as the crowd shouted, *"We have no Roman! Death to the traitors!"* After things calmed down the next day, Prignano accepts and twelve cardinals confirmed the election and enthroned him on April 18.

Urban began subjecting the French cardinals to abuse and created twenty new cardinals to eliminate the French majority. The papacy went to his head and his belligerent attitude and scandalous behavior made the authorities question his sanity. The

French cardinals collectively joined together and on August 2, declared the April election invalid *"as having been made, not freely, but under fear"* of mob violence, and invited Urban to abdicate. Seven days later, the French cardinals informed the whole Catholic world that the deranged and incapable Urban was deposed as an intruder.

The eleven French cardinals during the April conclave joined the six cardinals in Avignon and elected Robert of Geneva as Pope Clement VII on October 31. This was the beginning of the Great Schism, which lasted from 1378 to 1417 A.D. or 1429 A.D. depending on how one views it.

Europe had to decide between the *popes* who excommunicated each other.

Urban had to create a new curia because the old one sided with Clement. The mentally unstable Urban worked not to heal the schism but helped a worthless nephew gain control of the kingdom of Naples. He died on October 15, 1389 A.D. and was described as cruel and scandalous. The majority of the Church rejected him. However, St. Catherine of Sienna was his advocate and the Church later considered him the legitimate pope at the Council of Constance.

Clement VII was recognized as the true pope by the majority of the original cardinals and by many if not most Catholics in general. Charles V also recognized him, as did many of the monarchies around Europe except Germany and the eastern and Nordic countries. However, Clement, along with his Avignon successors, is considered invalid which gives them the label of antipopes on the official papal list.

Clement made sixteen-year-old Peter of Luxemburg bishop at Metz and then cardinal in 1384 A.D. Later, Peter was beatified in 1527 A.D. adding credibility to Clement's pontificate.

Clement excommunicated the successor of Urban, Boniface IX who was elected on November 2, 1389 A.D. Boniface also excommunicated Clement but had first offered him a chance to become legate to Spain and France if he would abdicate, but Clement obviously refused.

Boniface was notorious for his nepotism and made money by auctioning offices to the highest bidder, selling indulgences, and created jubilees by charging pilgrims for the journey and seeing of shrines. The future antipope John XXIII (Baldassare Cossa) helped Boniface finance the scandalous practices.

When Clement died on September 16, 1394 A.D., Pedro de Luna was elected September 28, taking the papal name Benedict XIII to continue the Avignon line. He was the last French cardinal to abandon Urban. Once he was convinced that he was not a true pope, he gave full support to Clement. As pope, Benedict was supported by Duke Louis of Orleans, but had to deal with fallout with his own countrymen.

He offered to meet Boniface to settle the schism but Boniface was not interested using health issues as an excuse not to meet. Before Boniface died in 1404 A.D., he had canonized Bridget of Sweden on October 7, 1391 A.D.

Benedict was a good man and strong in faith who wanted to end the schism. His good friend St. Vincent Ferrer, the greatest miracle worker the Catholic Church ever had, was at his side while acting as pope. Benedict tried to heal the schism with negotiations with Innocent VII who succeeded Boniface on October 17 1404 A.D. Innocent's election was opposed by the majority of Rome, but was admired for his strict spiritual life. He died on November 6, 1406 A.D.

**St. Vincent Ferrer preaching to the Moors (1350 – 1419 A.D.)
He rejected the papal claimant recognized by Rome, and helped
heal the Great Schism.**

Gregory XII succeeded Innocent on November 30, 1406 AD. Both he and Benedict wanted an end to the schism but both strongly believed each was the true pope. Negotiations were never made and the cardinals went to Pisa (without Benedict or Gregory because they refused to attend) and elected Alexander V on June 26, 1409 A.D.

The Catholic Church now had three men claiming to be the Roman Pontiff. It was impossible to decipher the best argument for each claim. Who was the true pope?

After Alexander rightly condemned John Wycliffe, he died suddenly five months later on May 3, 1410 A.D.

In the place of Alexander, Baldasar Cossa was elected May 17, 1410 A.D. taking the name John XXIII. His followers were well bribed and he was a scandal to the ages, utterly incapable of any office in the Church. He called a Council at Pisa, which condemned Wycliffe and Huss in 1413 A.D. He called another council at Constance in November 1414 A.D. but was deposed by the council on May 29, 1415 A.D., and died by poisoning November 22, 1419 A.D. He is considered an antipope, but his grave site says that he was once the pope.

Gregory XII abdicated during the Council of Constance on July 4, 1415 A.D. The same council deposed Benedict XIII July 26, 1417 A.D., who later died May 23, 1423 A.D. Benedict always believed he was the true pope and is considered the true pope by some today. His crosier and chalice are displayed in the local church and is remembered as Papa Luna. He is not on the official list of popes.

Martin V was elected to succeed Gregory on November 11, 1417 A.D. Clement VIII was elected June 10, 1423 A.D. to replace Benedict. He later abdicated on July 26, 1429 A.D. and recognized Martin V, thus ending the Great Schism. Some believe the schism ended after Benedict XIII was deposed and Martin was elected.

If reading this was a bit confusing, imagine living in it as a Catholic with the primitive methods of communication at that time.

The Implications

Between St. Catherine of Sienna and St. Vincent Ferrer, one and possibly both of these great saints were in serious error on which of the two sides had the true pope.

St. Catherine of Sienna and St. Vincent Ferrer

If the French cardinals were correct that they were not fully compliant in electing Urban due to fear, then his election should be considered null as with his successors Boniface, Innocent, and Gregory.

This would mean the official list got it backwards and should have placed the Avignon line as the true line of papal succession, which were Clement VII, Benedict XIII and Clement VIII.

Martin V would have started off as an antipope until Clement abdicated only then could Martin be considered a true pope.

However, this is not how history has viewed it. Regardless of the situation and facts, the Church wanted a true Roman line instead of seeing a valid Avignon line.

It is also possible that none of them were true popes until Martin V. I submit that all are at least doubtful popes for the exception of Martin V after the abdication and unification of Clement VIII. Therefore, none of them should be considered valid.

As we have seen in the chapters covering the first and the fifteenth anomalies, a long interregnum, even if it covered fifty years, would not contradict the doctrine, from the First Vatican Council, that by Divine Right, St. Peter has perpetual successors in the primacy over the universal Church

In 1882 A.D., Fr. Edmund James O'Reilly, an eminent Vatican approved theologian, in *The Relations of the Church to Society – Theological Essays,*" writes immediately after the First Vatican Council:

"We may here stop to inquire what is to be said of the position, at that time, of the three claimants, and their rights with regard to the Papacy. In the first place, there was all through, from the death of Gregory XI in 1378, a Pope – with the exception, of course, of the intervals between deaths and elections to fill up the vacancies thereby created. There was, I say, at every given time a Pope, really invested with the dignity of the Vicar of Christ and Head of the Church, whatever opinions might exist among many as to his genuineness; not that an interregnum covering the whole period would have been impossible or inconsistent with the promises of Christ, for this is by no means manifest, but that, as a matter of fact, there was not such an interregnum."

Though Fr. O'Reilly did not hold to an interregnum for the entire schism, he nonetheless taught that such an interregnum would not be impossible. In fact, Fr. O'Reilly gives this prophetic warning:

"The great schism of the West suggests to me a reflection which I take the liberty of expressing here. If this schism had not occurred, the hypothesis of such a thing happening would appear to many chimerical. They would say it could not be; God would not permit the Church to come into so unhappy a situation. Heresies might spring up and spread and last painfully long, through the fault and to the perdition of their authors and abettors, to the great distress too of the faithful, increased by actual persecution in many places where the heretics were dominant. But that the true Church should remain between thirty and forty years without a thoroughly ascertained Head, and representative of Christ on earth, this would not be. Yet it has been; and we have no guarantee that it will not be again, though we may fervently hope otherwise. What I would infer is, that we must not be too ready to pronounce on what God may permit. We know with absolute certainty that He will fulfill His promises... We may also trust that He will do a great deal more than what He has bound Himself by his promises. We may look forward with cheering probability to exemption for the future from some of the trouble and misfortunes that have befallen in the past. But we, or our successors in the future generations of Christians, shall perhaps see stranger evils than have yet been experienced, even before the immediate approach of that great winding up of all things on earth that will precede the day of judgment. I am not setting up for a prophet, nor pretending to see unhappy wonders, of which I have no knowledge whatever. All I mean to convey is that contingencies regarding the Church, not excluded by the Divine promises, cannot be regarded as practically impossible, just because they would be terrible and distressing in a very high degree."

This teaching is confirmed by Reverend M. P. Hill, S.J. (1915 A.D.): *"If during the entire* [Great] *schism there had been no*

Pope at all—that would not prove that the office and authority of Peter was not transmitted to the next Pope duly elected."

However, I submit that, indeed, the Great Schism was a long interregnum because all the popes during that time were questionable or doubtful. A doubtful pope cannot be a true pope. During that time, it was impossible for anyone to determine who the true pope was. Therefore, all of them must be considered at best doubtful, which makes all of them null and void.

If someone were to challenge the present position of sedevacantism by asking how it is possible for the church to be without a pope for fifty-plus years? The answer from the informed Catholic would be that it perhaps has done so before!

The Great Schism began at the election of Clement VII. If the Avignon claim had any legitimacy, which it did, then Urban V was the doubtful pope after his election on April 8, 1378 A.D. and the interregnum would last until 1429 A.D., a full fifty-one years later, when Clement VIII abdicated and joined Martin!

Throughout the Great Schism, bishops were consecrated and the sees were filled by supplied jurisdiction (comes from the Church) as ordinary jurisdiction (comes only from the pope) didn't truly exist during those years.

Fifteenth Century painting of Joan of Arc who was burned at the stake May 30, 1431 A.D. at nineteen years of age. She was born during the time when three *popes* reigned at the same time. (*Centre Historique des Archives Nationales*, Paris, AE II 2490)

Nineteenth Anomaly:

Alexander VI Buys the Papacy

Simony has been a serious problem within the Church for many years. This abuse entails the exchange, for a temporal price, of those things that are spiritual. Simony, as it applies specifically to this anomaly, is the acquirement of a spiritual office monetarily or by things of worth and power such as property.

The term itself is properly named after the magician Simon Magus found in the Book of Acts, chapter 8, who attempted to buy the gift of bestowing the Holy Ghost by the laying of hands, to confer the Sacrament of Confirmation.

"And when Simon saw that, by the imposition of the hands of the apostles, the Holy Ghost was given, he offered them money, Saying: Give me also this power, that on whomsoever I shall lay my hands, he may receive the Holy Ghost. But Peter said to him: Keep thy money to thyself, to perish with thee: because thou hast thought that the gift of God may be purchased with money. Thou hast no part or lot in this matter. For thy heart is not right in the sight of God."

Simony was so frowned upon by the Church that...

Pope Nicholas II, presiding at the Roman Synod in the Basilica of Constantine (1060 A.D.), pronounced: *"We judge that in preserving dignity no mercy is to be shown toward the simoniacs; but according to the sanctions of the canons and decrees of the Holy Fathers we condemn them entirely and by apostolic authority we decree that they are to be deposed... Thus, moreover, by the authority of the holy Apostles Peter and Paul we entirely forbid that at any time any of our successors from this our permission take or fix a rule for himself or another, because the authority of the ancient Fathers has not promulgated this by order or grant, but too great a necessity of the time has force us to permit it..."*

Pope Pascal II at the Council of Guastalla (1106 A.D.) declared that any bishop from a schismatic and heretical group would be accepted in the episcopal offices except for those proven to be usurpers, simoniacs, and criminals.

Pope Innocent II sharply denounced simony in several canons at the Second Lateran Council in 1139 A.D.

Pope Alexander III in 1179 A.D. at the Third Lateran Council decreed, *"Chap. 10. Let monks not be received in the monastery at a price...If anyone, however, on being solicited gives anything for his reception, let him not advance to sacred orders. Let him, however, who accepts (a price) be punished by the taking away of his office."* A subtitle remarked, *"Thus also Urban II in the Synod of Melfi 1089 A.D., c. 8 [Msi XX 723 C]."*

Then came along Rodrigo de Borgia; the pope who'll be notoriously remembered as one of the unholiest popes in history. The Borgia name was already well-known as Rodrigo's maternal uncle was Pope Callistus III. Rodrigo was handsome and debonair. His uncle, the pope, made him a cardinal-deacon and vice-chancellor of the Holy See. His name and position provided him with oodles of gold. He became the second richest cardinal and one of the wealthiest men in the world.

Although Rodrigo was a crack administrator, he had one major downfall: the lust for women. In 1460 A.D., Pope Pius II severely reprimanded him for participating in a public orgy in Sienna which caused a great scandal among the people. However, it didn't stop ole' Rodrigo from being a player. He continued in unchaste ways, eventually hooking up with Vanozza Catanei who bore his four children. They would later be involved in his papacy.

Ten years after the birth of his fourth child, and eight days after Christopher Columbus set sail to the New World, Rodrigo de

Borgia bought the papacy with outright bribery and promised riches, taking the name Alexander VI on August 11, 1492 A.D.

As pope, he made the young Giulia *the beautiful* Farnese his long time mistress. She became known in some circles as the pope's whore. Through her relationship with Alexander, her brother Alessandro was made a cardinal. Cardinal Alessandro later became Pope Paul III on October 13, 1534 A.D.

As a distraction from his sexual misconduct, Alexander reformed several aspects of the Church. One of Alexander's notable acts was the drawing of the line of demarcation in the New World between Spain and Portugal in 1493 A.D.

A year later, King Charles VIII of France, with the support of Cardinal Giuliano della Rovere (later Pope Julius II), attempted to cross the Alps and depose Alexander for simony but their efforts failed.

The following year another brave man would stand against Alexander, Dominican Father Girolamo Savonarola. He was a staunch defender of orthodoxy and holiness. Savonarola wrote a poem titled, *"On the Decline of the Church,"* describing the depravity of the Renaissance Era. Filled with intense zeal for the salvation of mankind, his powerful sermons changed those Florentines that loved and lived as pagans. He inspired the bonfire of the vanities that took place February 7, 1497 A.D., in which the inhabitants of the city took all the mirrors, bad books, cosmetics, and anything else that could become an occasion of sin and burned them in a great pile. Also attributed to Savonarola is the second part of the *Ave Maria* first seen in written form and found in his *"Esposizione sopra l'Ave Maria."*

Girolamo Savonarola, 1497 A.D., Fra Bartolomeo (1472 – 1517 A.D.) Florence, *Museo di San Marco*

Sometime between the years of 1494 and 1495 A.D., Girolamo Savonarola denounced Alexander for simony, which according to the former, invalidated the election of Alexander thus making him an antipope. Alexander never denied the accusation that he bought the papacy; he knew Savonarola spoke the truth. It was no real secret. At the conclave, Cardinal Francesco Todeschini, later Pope Pius III, infuriately rejected a bribe in voting for Alexander.

Prideful Alexander excommunicated Savonarola on May 12, 1497 A.D. in the bull *Cum saepenumero*, but the Dominican rejected the bull as invalid being the antipope Alexander was. Knowing that a good defense is a good offense, Alexander set out to destroy the man of God altogether. Reverend Savonarola, along with two other priests, was imprisoned, tortured, and finally hanged on May 23, 1498 A.D. They were burned entirely and their ashes dumped into the river Arno to prevent relics from being collected. Alexander VI and his son Caesar will be poisoned five years later.

As evil as Alexander was in his time, one can still find defenders of him while Savonarola is looked upon as a disobedient false prophet who fell into schism. Compare this, however, with the great Catholic saints who came along and saw Savonarola as a servant of truth and justice.

Savonarola would somewhat be vindicated by the next two popes. First, Pius III (nephew of Pope Pius II) was a witness to Alexander's simony. Unfortunately, he died less than a month after his election. Another witness to the simoniacal election was Pope Julius II, whose thwarted plot to oust Alexander for simony, had remained hidden in fear of assassination from the *"pope"*. Once pope himself, Pope Julius II would condemn simony in the bull *Cum tam divino* in 1513 A.D. He said that any ecclesial office, including the papacy, would be null and void if obtained by simony.

However, the bull would be ignored a mere ten years later when the rich Guilio de' Medici (Pope Clement VII, the second pope with who took this name) distributed sixty-thousand ducats among the conclave cardinals to be elected November 19, 1523 A.D. He had even persuaded Holy Roman Emperor Charles V of Spain to help out and when Clement later betrayed him, Charles remarked how he regrettably poured out streams of gold to get him elected.

The late Father Malachi Martin wrote that, *"He* [Clement VII] *had bought Cardinal Colonna's vote with a palace and the chancellorship, Cardinal Carnaro's with the Palace of San Marco, and the infamous Cardinal Soderini's with total amnesty for Soderini's heinous crimes, including several murders."* Clement VII's questionable pontificate was also a total disaster; one of the worst ever.

Be that as it may, Dominican Father Girolamo Savonarola, with many miracles attributed to his name, was venerated by later great saints such as: St. Philip Neri, St. Catherine Ricci, St. John Fisher, and the great Pope St. Pius V, and Pope St. Pius X.

Hanging and burning of Girolamo Savonarola in *Piazza della Signoria* in Florence in 1498 A.D. Anonymous painting from 1498 A.D., in the *Museo di San Marco*, Florence.

The Implications

The Church recognizes as popes those who acquired the office monetarily despite the prohibition of Church law at the time of Alexander VI, which actually spells out nullity and deposal in such cases.

Although Alexander is considered a true pope, and listed as such on the official list, it appears that Savonarola was correct. The Divine law of God obviously prohibits the buying of the papacy. How it affects the papacy is a matter of ecclesiastical (Church) law. The bull of Pope Julius II wouldn't necessarily apply during the time of the Apostle St. Peter. However, the pronouncement of Pope Nicholas II in 1060 A.D. does apply in the case of Alexander and he should have been deposed before his election. Pope Julius II knew this and so, with the help of secular powers, unsuccessfully attempted to depose Alexander.

The bull of Pope Julius II, declaring null and void any papal election acquired by simony, however, was rescinded by Pope St. Pius X in Constitution, *Vacante Sede,* issued December 25, 1904. Later, on December 8, 1945 A.D., Pope Pius XII's Constitution, *Vacantis Apostolicae Sedis*, reinforced Pope St. Pius V's reform. Pius XII's constitution in part (6) states, *"Simony, whether of the divine or the human law, in the election is condemned under pain of excommunication, but not under pain of invalidity of the election, so that the validity of the election of the Pope cannot be attacked by anyone on this pretext."*

In other words, the election would be valid even if simony were present, but those involved, including the newly elected pope would be under the pain of excommunication. The phrase *"Under pain of excommunication"* is merely a threat. Those involved would not actually be excommunicated unless declared so. Church prelates could follow-up on the threat and excommunicate those involved such as cardinals, etc, unless the delinquent is the pope. No authority on earth can excommunicate him. However, the pope who acquired the papal office via simony would be in mortal sin and he would be expected to renounce his pontificate and beg forgiveness from God and the Church. All his acts as pope would be sinful, and the faithful would need to avoid him if possible. Therefore, one can buy the Throne of Peter, but it would be to the detriment of his eternal soul.

The new constitutions made provisions to prevent anyone from rejecting future elections on the pretext of simony, which might cause confusion and schism. Not that anything was wrong with the past law of Pope Julius II, but laws may change for whatever reason the Church deems to be more appropriate for the time.

However, no Church law was in place when other *"popes"* perhaps bought the papacy. The cases of Benedict IX and Gregory VI (whose pontificates were discussed in the twelfth anomaly) most certainly fall under the condemnations of Divine law, if not Church law. Both men committed mortal sins. When Pope Nicholas II pronounced that simoniacs be deposed, without doubt, he was influenced by the atrocious examples of his immediate predecessors and the common practice of simony in his day.

In the Divine Comedy, the great poet Dante placed Nicholas III in hell buried upside down, the soles of his feet burning with oil, thus mocking baptism, due to simony. Nicholas tells Dante that Pope Boniface VIII was also in hell for the sin of simony. Dante seems to imply that Clement V was guilty of simony and therefore in hell. The real reason why Dante may have placed Clement V in hell was because he transferred the papacy to Avignon, France and outside of Dante's native Italy, which for any Italian would be considered a mortal sin. However, if what Dante alludes to in his poem is true, that these men were guilty of simony, then they shouldn't have had any real right to the papacy by law.

During the time of Savonarola, such provisions found in the twentieth century constitutions were not in place, and the declaration by Pope Nicholas II in 1060 A.D. ordered simoniacs to be deposed. How is it possible that Savonarola was wrong under the law in his time?

Again, it should be noted that Pope St. Leo IX would reordain men who were previously ordained by known simoniac bishops. This was because St. Leo believed that some simoniac bishops were not valid or their consecrations were considered doubtful or invalid. In 1053 A.D., St. Peter Damiani wrote the treatise, *Liber Gratissimus*, defending the validity of Orders by simoniacs. However, that question was not answered definitively by the Church until the Second Lateran Council under Pope Innocent II in 1139 A.D., which affirmed the validity but the illicitness of the sacrament.

However, the question is not about the validity of the sacrament, but the validity of the papal office. As discussed on page 50, the sacrament will always be valid provided the essential elements are present as defined by Pope Eugene IV, at the Council of Florence in Session 8, on November 22, 1439 A.D. in *Exultate Deo*: *"All these sacraments are made up of three elements: namely, things as the matter, words as the form, and the person of the minister who confers the sacrament with the intention of doing what the Church does. If any of these is lacking, the sacrament is not effected."*

The validity of the papal office would depend on the law of the Church at the time. When Alexander burst onto the scene, the Church required deposal for simoniacs. Notwithstanding, the whole Church seems to recognize Alexander VI as a true pope but a bad one.

I submit that Alexander was at best a doubtful pope and Savonarola was right in declaring him as having no right to the papacy.

Also, Clement VII's pontificate came after the bull of Pope Julius II. If papal bulls are to mean anything, Clement VII's election should be considered null and void regardless.

Twentieth Anomaly:

The Great Apostasy

God has allowed all of the previous anomalies to prepare us for this devastating one. When all the previous implications are grasped, the transition to the great apostasy will be uncomplicated and easier to acknowledge. The reason why this anomaly takes place to begin with is due to an unhealthy attitude and misunderstanding of the papacy as it is properly represented in the introduction of this book.

We begin in the nineteenth century when modernism began to creep into the Church. The core belief of modernism has as its foundation, *"that what was true yesterday is not necessarily true today."* The great apostasy has modernism as its foundation since truth is redefined by what is true for the moment. In other words, modernism is the belief that doctrine and truth evolve because truth is not immutable.

The modernist could logically contradict himself throughout time, since his system of belief holds that at one point in time a doctrine can be true, but at another point in time ceasing to be true. This *"new truth"* for the modernist becomes nothing more than a convenient truth for the moment.

After Pope Pius IX condemned elements of modernism in the Syllabus of Errors on December 8, 1864 A.D., Pope St. Pius X disclosed the document *Lamentabili Sane Exitu*, in July 1907 A.D. which comprehensively condemned sixty-five propositions as pertaining to modernism. Later in September of the same year, St. Pius X promulgated an encyclical *Pascendi dominici gregis* which enjoined a mandatory *Oath Against Modernism* on all Catholic clergy and teachers. In the encyclical, St. Pius X denounced modernism as the *"synthesis of all heresies"* because this new system of belief allows for the interjection of whatever man wants to hold as true.

Pope Pius IX and Pope St. Pius X

The condemnations by Pope St. Pius X were the hallmark of his pontificate. They would fall on deaf ears in the years to come.

In the 1958 A.D., Angelo Giuseppe Roncalli was the beginning of the end for the Roman Church. He took the name John XXIII; the same name as the antipope Baldasar Cossa found in the eighteenth anomaly. Three months later, he gave notice that he would call another council. It would be the death blow to Rome.

The similarities between the two *"popes"* are staggering. The reign of the first John XXIII lasted five years as did the second John XXIII. The first John XXIII called the Council of Constance, and the second John XXIII called the Second Vatican Council. The first John XXIII opened his council in the fourth year of his reign and the second John XXIII opened his council in the fourth year of his reign. The first John XXIII died just before the third session of his council, and the second John XXIII died just before the third session of his council.

In mid October 1958 A.D., Vatican insider and the first Catholic *sedevacantist*, Dr. Elizabeth Gerstner leaked the information that Roncalli was to be elected in the next conclave. It was all planned.

"There was, however, a German journalist, Elisabeth Gerstner, who smelled the truth in the air and, risking accusations of insanity, wrote it and hit the mark. In an article titled "Zur Todesstunde Pius XII" appeared on the "General Anzeiger für den Nieder-Rhein" by mid-October 1958, Gerstner wrote in detail, that the Conclave would elect Venice's patriarch Roncalli, who would open the door to the future Paul VI (4)." Reference : Nikita Roncalli by Franco Bellegrandi published in Italian in 1994 A.D.

Dr. Gerstner had also warned her friends that Roncalli, Montini (later Paul VI), and Ratzinger (later Benedict XVI) belonged to a little homosexual group ready to alter the Church in their time.

Roncalli was practically raised as a modernist. During his youth, he was involved in the youth organization *"Opera Dei Congress"* that was dissolved by Pope St. Pius X for modernism. He was later associated with notorious modernists such as Bishop Radini Tedeschi, Bishop Carlo Ferrara of Milan, Bishop Bonomello of Cremona, and Lamberdo Beauduin. Even his closest seminary friends including roommate (later Bishop of Bergamo) who assisted at his ordination were excommunicated for modernism.

When he was a Professor of Patristics at the Lateran University, he was removed *"on suspicion of modernism"* and for teaching the theories of Rudolf Steiner, an illuminati member and originator of *"The Science of the Spirit known as Anthroposophy."* A file dated to 1925 A.D., the Holy Office had maintained a dossier on Angelo Roncalli which read *"suspected of Modernism."* Roncalli removed it when he gained power.

Angelo Roncalli, aka, Pope John XXIII

When elevated to the College of Cardinals, Roncalli insisted upon receiving the red hat from Vincent Auriol, President of the Masonic *"Fourth Republic"* of France.

French police appointed to guard him during his nunciature in Paris testified that he would attend every Thursday evening in civilian clothes the Grand Lodge of Freemasonry.

In the late 1940's A.D., Roncalli was initiated into the Freemasons along with Montini. His good friend and notorious thirty-third degree Scottish Rite Freemason Baron Yves Marsaudon claims that Roncalli also became a thirty-third degree Mason while a nuncio at France. It was here that Roncalli appointed Marsaudon, as head of the French branch of the Knights of Malta, a Catholic lay order, causing a major scandal. Baron Marsaudon would praise Roncalli throughout his pontificate for calling the Second Vatican Council that reflected their Masonic ideals.

As "*pope*"he broke all papal traditions. He wrote a Masonic type of encyclical *"Pacem et Terris"* and was praised by the Communists and Freemasons. When necessary he simply contradicted previous popes. He rejected in toto Gregory XVI's *Mirari vos* and *Singulari nos*, and the *Quanta cura* of Pius IX, to which was attached, as appendix, *The Syllabus of Errors*. John was ruthless in dismissing the views of his predecessors. When asked about following in the footsteps of so great a man as Pius XII, John XXIII responded, *"I try to imagine what my predecessor would have done, and then I do just the opposite."*

Roncalli would continue the revolution by revising the mass and eliminating many traditional prayers. He completely altered the calendar by removing many great saints. He was relentless in change, but not as much so as his predecessors.

One of his first acts was to make Giovanni Baptiste Montini (his papal successor Paul VI) a cardinal, something Pope Pius XII refused to do after it was found Montini had been secretly communicating with Stalin during World War II. Promoting Montini to the cardinalate positioned him to become *"Pope"*Paul VI, which was apparently the game plan all along, as suggested by a 1956 A.D. *LIFE* magazine's edition when he was still only a bishop. The prediction obviously came to pass.

Giovanni Battista Montini sealed the fate for the Church in Rome. He took the name of Paul VI in 1963 A.D. His mother was a convert from Judaism. Her funeral monument has Masonic symbols engraved all over it. They are so blatant that a wall was built in front of it to hide them.

Jesuit Father, Doctor of Theology, Church history, Canon law, and one of the first Catholic *sedevacantists*, Fr. Joaquin Saenz Y Arriaga, S.J. wrote how the Montini family is listed in the *Golden Book of Noble Italian Heritage* (1962-1964 A.D., p. 994): *"A branch of the... noble family from Brescia... wherefrom their noble blazon comes and which avows as its sure trunk and* founder, a Bartholomew (Bartolino) de Benedictis, said Montini was of Hebrew origin. "Interestingly enough, there is no record of Baptism for Giovanni Montini.

Montini was known in his seminary days as a notorious homosexual, which of course, explains his involvement with Roncalli and Ratzinger as told by the late Dr. Gerstner. As the saying goes, birds of a feather flock together would be realized throughout their new church in the years to come when over fifty percent of all priests would be Sodomites. That's no coincidence.

In 1944 A.D., Montini worked with the Soviets through a childhood friend Togliatti, who was head of the Communist party in Italy. The Archbishop Primate of the Protestant church in Sweden, who was a state official, informed Pope Pius XII of the situation. It came as a shock to Pius XII who exiled Montini to Milan without the traditional red hat. Investigations into Montini's Soviet affair resulted in finding that his private secretary, the Jesuit Tondi, was a KGB agent who was once the Professor of Atheism at the University of Maxism-Leninism. Tondi gave the Soviets the names of all the clergy sent to Russia who were immediately caught and executed. Tondi was imprisoned and later married his mistress, the militant Communist Carmen Zanti in a civil service. After Montini's election to the papacy, Tondi returned to Rome to work in the Vatican's Civil Service as a cover for his KGB activities. Paul VI was greeted on the balcony after his papal *"election"* with cries of *"il Papa Montinovsky."*

Paul VI was a communist sympathizer. The Pact of Metz held in 1962 A.D., guaranteed that the Vatican would not condemn communism at the Second Vatican Council. However, earlier in 1942 A.D., talks already were in the works with Communist Moscow. The late Fr. Malachi Martin wrote that, *"It was in that year, that Vatican Monsignor Giovanni Battista Montini, who himself later succeeded to the Papacy as Paul VI, talked directly with Joseph Stalin's representative. Those talks were aimed at dimming Pius XII's constant fulminations against the Soviet dictator and Marxism. Stato himself had been privy to those talks. He had also been privy to the conversations between Montini and the Italian Communist Party leader, Palmiro Togliatti, in 1944 .... "Stato offered to supply reports from the Allied Office of Strategic Services about the matter, beginning, as he recalled, with OSS Report JR-1022 of August 28, 1944."*

Mark Winckler, interpreter working at the Vatican, tells of a meeting he had with Cardinal Pignedoli (then Msgr.). Pignedoli told him in 1944 A.D. that the failed Freemasonic plan to have Cardinal Rampolla elected pope in 1903 A.D. would be corrected when they elect Montini.

With Roncalli in Paris, Montini was initiated into the Freemasonic brotherhood in the late 1940's A.D. Baron Marsaudon would also praise Montini for not only continuing the revolution of John XXIII, but taking it further and completing it as his own.

Montini didn't disappoint his modernist Masonic brotherhood. He literally changed everything in the Church because as he said, *"If the world changes, should not religion also change? ...Everything must change, everything must progress. Evolution seems to be the law that brings liberation. There must be a great deal that is true and good in this mentality..."*

The Masonic plans were, of course, to infiltrate the Church until one of their own became pope, knowing full well that obedience will be given to him. Thus, the Masonic doctrines will be held as Catholic orthodoxy. The Masons have planned and boasted about it for over a century. With full knowledge by the Church about the plan, the Masons were still able to accomplish their goals. That goal particularly was to change Catholicism to conform to the world. In other words, the Church is no longer to be countercultural. So when Montini is elected as Paul VI, he finishes the work that began under John XXIII and undoes the historic faith and replaces it with the new modernist Masonic religion usurping the Catholic name.

The Second Vatican Council approved and ratified by Paul VI would declare that Muslims worship the one and same true God as Catholics even though they reject God in Christ. It declared that man has a right to be wrong in the public arena. And if that weren't enough, it redefined what makes up the Catholic Church contradicting all the popes in the past.

During the council, on November 13, 1964 A.D., Paul VI gave away the triple-crowned papal tiara which symbolized the pope's authority. Paul VI had the tiara auctioned at the New York World's Fair.

Paul VI gave his Shepherd's Crook and Fisherman's Ring to U Thant, head of the UN, who sold them to a Jewish businessman in the Midwest. He abolished the rite of Tonsure, all four Minor Orders (invalidly replacing two), and the rank of subdiaconate. He abolished the *Oath Against Modernism*, at a time when modernism was everywhere. After all, modernism was the very foundation for the new religion of Rome.

Paul VI gave back to the Muslims the Standard of Lepanto. The flag represented the Christian naval defeat of the Muslim invasion into Europe in 1571 A.D. It was originally taken from a Turkish admiral in the great naval battle of Lepanto. Pope St. Pius V commanded fasting and the praying of the Rosary before the great test of an outnumbered Christian fleet. The pope honored God with the victory by instituting the Feast Day to His Mother, Our Lady of the Most Holy Rosary. In giving back the standard, Paul VI was renouncing and apologizing for the Christian victory and sacrifice.

Following the Second Vatican Council, Paul VI changed all seven of the sacraments, four which contradicted past solemn papal definitions on what made the sacraments valid. He appointed the Freemason priest Annibali Bugnini including six Protestants to concoct the *'novus ordo missae'* (the new mass) which changed the very words of Christ during the most solemn consecration. Contrary to the teaching of St. Paul and the entire history of Christianity, Paul VI allowed women to read from the Holy Scriptures as lectors. The new religion of Rome began with its new laws, new practices, new worship ceremony, and new doctrines. Despite all past papal condemnations, Montini would praise and recognize as legitimate all the false religions and their leaders around the world in expectation that his followers would do the same.

Giovanni Battista Montini, aka, Pope Paul VI

Paul VI removed forty more saints from the new liturgical calendar. He removed solemn exorcisms from the baptismal rite. He harmfully changed solemn exorcisms. He approved the translation and use of the radical modernist *New American Bible* which explains in the introduction and footnotes that the Holy

Gospels were not inspired by God and contradicted one another in reality rather than just in appearance.

All this change came under the guise of papal authority under papal infallibility, which made the Masonic Plan a success. Only fifty years earlier did Pope St. Pius X warn of these very events as the Masonic Plan was made public.

If the initial plan wasn't sinister enough, the exorcist priest Father Malachi Martin reported that on June 29, 1963 A.D., the night before Paul VI's coronation, a black mass was celebrated and Satan was enthroned in the Vatican! Fr. Malachi has confirmed this fact several times in interviews and has believed the Vatican has been possessed by Satan ever since.

On November 21, 1970 A.D., Paul VI also excluded all cardinals over eighty years of age from participating in papal elections fixing the next conclave from allowing any sort of a counter-reformation from old orthodox cardinals still living. It worked perfectly. The 78' conclave was stacked. John had appointed eight cardinals and Paul had appointed one hundred cardinals out of the one hundred eleven that voted.

In 1978 A.D., Albino Luciani, was elected and chose the name, John Paul. He was made bishop by John XXIII, and a cardinal by Paul VI.

Never before in history did a pope attempt take a double name. He took the two names of his predecessors as if they were his mentors approving of the disaster that had taken place in the last twenty years. John Paul continued the affliction of his predecessors by promoting the Second Vatican Council. However, it wouldn't last long. He died thirty-three days after his election.

With the conclave stacked again, Polish Cardinal Karol Jozef Wojtyla was the next in line after the short reign of John Paul I. He would take the same name as his predecessor and for the same reasons. He was also made a cardinal by Paul VI.

In October 1962 A.D., Bishop Wojtyła made two influential contributions to the Second Vatican Council: *The Decree on Religious Freedom* (*Dignitatis Humanae*) and *The Pastoral Constitution on the Church in the Modern World* (*Gaudium et Spes*).

John Paul II's *"pontificate"* was ostentatious. He continued the radical liberalism of his three predecessors. He appointed notorious modernist theologians to the College of Cardinals such as French priest, Henry de Lubac, and allowed the modernist priest Raymond Brown to head the Pontifical Biblical Commission never once censoring him. He continued the feminist revolution of Paul VI allowing women to serve in the sanctuary which was condemned as an evil practice by at least three previous popes. In serving the new mass, John Paul II would concelebrate the Divine Liturgy with Eastern heretics and schismatics which had been forbidden in both Divine and Church law. He also participated in non-Catholic worship services, such as the Anglicans and Lutherans, which also break the same Divine and Church laws, but John Paul II didn't stop there.

In 1985 A.D., John Paul II prayed *"with"* African Animists known as *"witch doctors."* On February 5, 1986 A.D., in the city of Chennai (Madras for the Zoroastrians) India, John Paul II, alongside Dr. Meher Master Moos, actively participated in a pagan Zoroastrian ceremony by lighting a candle as he wore a stole with the symbols of the pagan religion.

Two months later in a synagogue, he would actively take part in a Jewish ceremony. Not surprising then to see him praying at the Wailing Wall which was the left over remnant of the 70 A.D. destruction of Jerusalem as the just punishment God inflicted on the rebellious Jewish people.

The following year in Phoenix, Arizona, John Paul II said that the ritual blessing he received, from the Pima Indian shaman Emmet White using an eagle's feather, had enriched the Church.

On February 5, 1986 A.D., in the city of Chennai (Madras for the Zoroastrians) India, John Paul II, alongside Dr. Meher Master Moos, actively participated in a Zoroastrian ceremony by lighting a candle as he wore a stole with the symbols of the pagan religion.

In 1986 and 2002 A.D., John Paul II invited all the world's religious leaders to come to Assisi, Italy and pray and offer sacrifices to each of their individual gods for world peace. Leaders from Eastern Orthodoxy, Protestantism, Judaism, Islam, Buddhism, Hinduism, Tenrikyo, Shintoism, Sikhism, Zoroastrianism, and Voodoo attended with prayers and even with animal sacrifices from the Voodooists all in the name of peace.

John Paul II also praised and promoted the Islamic culture. He once asked God to protect the religion through the intercession of St. John the Baptist. On February 4, 1993 A.D., he actually promoted the African religion of Voodooism implying that man may be saved in Voodoo. His promotion of non-Christian religions wouldn't be complete until he praised all the false religions of paganism, which of course he did on November 7, 1999 A.D. during the Pan-Christian Encounter in the center of St. Peter's Square.

In the 1980's A.D., John Paul II received awards and honors from the B'nai B'rith (Jewish Freemasonry) for his promotion of the Jewish people and their religion. In December of 1996 A.D., the Grand Orient Lodge of Italian Freemasonry offered John Paul II its greatest honor, the Order of Galilee, as an expression of thanks for the efforts that he made in support of Freemasonic ideals. The representative of Italian Freemasonry noted that John Paul II merited the honor because he had promoted *"the values of universal Freemasonry: fraternity, respect for the dignity of man, and the spirit of tolerance, central points of the life of true masons."*

On January 11, 1989 A.D., John Paul II would deny the historic understanding and belief of the Catholic dogma and Article of Faith of Christ's Descent into Hell by claiming that it was all just a metaphor.

October 11, 1992 A.D., he issued the new catechism of the Catholic Church which omits all references to Pope St. Pius X's condemnations of modernism.

In John Paul II's hallmark encyclical, *Evangelium vitae* (1995 A.D.), he implies that the historic Catholic teaching and practice of the death penalty was immoral and unjust. According to John Paul II, the death penalty is justified only when it defends public order and ensuring people's safety, and such cases where men cannot be kept from being a threat to society are, of course, practically non-existent.

In the past, the Catholic Church has officially and universally taught by Popes Julius II, Leo X, and St. Pius V that the practice of the death penalty for sodomites was a just punishment because the abomination of the sin required retribution against the holy Name and Authority of God. Ensuring public order is secondary. The reason the death penalty was required in the Old Testament was because the holiness of God outweighs the dignity of human life.

However, the new religion of John Paul II doesn't recognize the superiority of God's dignity over man's dignity. Both are recognized as being equal. In other words, Rome raised the level of man's dignity equal to God with the teaching that the love of God and neighbor are one and the same. Modernist Rome has necessarily rejected the historic teaching and practice of the Catholic Church. *Evangelium vitae* is a typical modernist document since truth yesterday is not true today.

John Paul II would at the end of his life add five new decades to the rosary. He apparently didn't think the Virgin Mary had perfected the form for the rosary as the Church had it for past seven hundred years. He called his new decades the luminous mysteries. These mysteries are now said by *Novus Ordo Catholics* on Thursdays in place of the traditional Joyful Mysteries.

By the time John Paul II died in 2005 A.D., the world had become so enamored in liberalism and modernism that the next elected *"pope"* would be considered theologically conservative. In reality, however, the liberalism of the next man, who would be placed as head of the new church at Rome, would continue the destruction of Christianity. That man would be Joseph Alois Ratzinger, aka, Benedict XVI.

Ratzinger was made a bishop in 1977 A.D. under the new rite of Orders and Paul VI made him cardinal in the same year. Like John XXIII, Ratzinger is on official Church record for suspect of heresy. Like John XXIII and Paul VI before him, Ratzinger is recognized by some Catholics as a homosexual.

From 1962 to 1965 A.D., he made a notable contribution to Vatican II as an *"expert"* being present at the council as theological advisor of Cardinal Joseph Frings, Archbishop of

Cologne. He was viewed during the time of the council as a reformer, cooperating with radical modernist theologians like Hans Kung and Edward Schillebeeckx. Ratzinger was an admirer of Karl Rahner, a notorious liberal/modernist theologian and a proponent of church reform. At the council, Ratzinger is pictured wearing at a suit and tie with Rahner, also in suit and tie.

Ratzinger admitted to being a liberal during the days of the Second Vatican Council and in an interview 1993 A.D. said his views had not changed one iota since that time. In 1990 A.D. and 1995 A.D., Ratzinger would confess over and over that he was the same liberal as in his days during the council.

30 Dias - July, 1990 A.D., Father Ratzinger attends Vatican II in a suit and tie with the liberal Fr Karl Rahner, also in suit and tie.

In 1972 A.D. together with Hans Urs von Balthasar, Henri de Lubac and other important theologians, he initiated the theological journal *"Communio."* This was the mouthpiece of the New Theology, officially condemned by Pope Pius XII, as being nothing but a heap of *"false opinions, which threaten to overthrow the very foundations of Catholic doctrine,"* and had now become according to Fr. Henrici, *"the official theology of Vatican II."*

Ratzinger wrote that the teachings of the past popes against modernism were now obsolete. He wrote that dogmatic formulas must constantly change.

After his *"election"*, Benedict XVI has maintained that he will give his full and complete support and promote the novelties of Vatican II. His first appointment was San Francisco's Archbishop Levada to the head of the Congregation for the Doctrine of Faith. Levada is on record for supporting homosexual rights and benefits. He was accused of covering two priests charged with molesting boys.

Ratzinger continued to make many staggering remarks in word and deed contradicting the historic Catholic Faith. A few such examples would include celebrating the twentieth anniversary of the abominable Assisi Events stating that *"in all great religious traditions"* there is a *"close bond that exists between the relationship with God and the ethics of love."*

On Jan. 16, 2006 A.D., he wished Chief Rabbi of Rome well in his mission against Christ. The second meeting with Rowan Williams, Archbishop of Canterbury, in 2008 A.D., Benedict XVI asked the Lord to promote the heresy of Anglicanism.

He would follow in the footsteps of his hero John Paul II and participate in a Jewish ceremony in a synagogue on August 19, 2005 A.D. At the height of Islamic terror on the world, on November 30, 2006 A.D., Benedict XVI prayed in a mosque with Muslims as Muslims (barefoot with arms crossed) towards Mecca.

Like his predecessors, he blesses and promotes the United Nations leading the charge for the New World Order. Benedict is the embodiment of Vatican II. Nothing seems to stop the onslaught of the New-Ager of Rome from turning the world into one giant brothel of heathenism.

On November 30, 2006 A.D., Benedict XVI prayed in a mosque with Muslims as Muslims (barefoot with arms crossed) towards Mecca.

The day before Ratzinger entered the conclave that elected him on April 19, 2005 A.D., he stated,

"We must not remain children in faith, in the condition of minors. And what does it mean to be children in faith? St Paul answers: it means being "tossed here and there, carried about by every wind of doctrine" (Eph 4: 14). This description is very timely!

How many winds of doctrine have we known in recent decades, how many ideological currents, how many ways of thinking. The small boat of the thought of many Christians has often been tossed about by these waves – flung from one extreme to another: from Marxism to liberalism, even to atheism to a vague religious mysticism; from agnosticism to syncretism and so forth. Every day new sects spring up, and what St. Paul says about human deception and the trickery that strives to entice people into error (cf. Eph 4:14) comes true.

Today, having a clear faith based on the Creed of the Church is often labeled as fundamentalism. Whereas relativism, that is, letting oneself be "tossed here and there, carried about by every wind of doctrine", seems the only attitude that can cope with modern times. We are building a dictatorship of relativism that does not recognize anything as definitive and whose ultimate goal consists solely of one's own ego and desires."

That's the pot calling the kettle black, just a different shade. No better way to fool the faithful of its own modernism than to condemn the world of its relativism. Ratzinger was condemning himself and his own religion for it surely is one of the new *winds of doctrine* that sprang up a new sect under the Second Vatican Council. That *human deception and trickery that strives to entice people into error* was at its best with Ratzinger preaching his hypocritical homily.

When the faithful wonder how the teachings of Vatican II square-up with historic Catholicism, they're to check in their brains at the front door, and view a continuity to the obvious contradictions that exist with the documents of the council and the historic Faith. It didn't fool John Paul I. He had attended the Second Vatican Council and afterwards made the statement, *"the Church had always taught that only the truth had rights, but now the Council made it clear that error also has rights."*

If the Catholic Church has always taught something, then it falls under the universal and ordinary magisterium. Thus, it is infallible and the full assent of faith is to be given by the faithful. John Paul I's admission proves that Vatican II contradicts the Catholic Faith. All bishops at Vatican II that signed the documents, with full knowledge to what they were signing, anathematized themselves and immediately lost their authority and jurisdiction. It didn't matter though, because the council was a major success for the modernists as the long-planned, two-part Masonic scheme took effect in Rome. The majority of faithful bought into and accepted, without question, a Masonic pope and the decrees of Masonic doctrine. Behold, the great apostasy foretold in Holy Scripture epiphanised.

Today, John XXIII, Paul VI, John Paul I, and John Paul II are considered heroes of the Catholic Church they usurped. On September 3, 2000, John Paul II beatified John XXIII as *"Blessed"* in heaven. On December 19, 2009 A.D., Benedict signed a decree recognizing John Paul II's life as one led in heroic virtue, giving his predecessor the title *"Venerable"*. At this present point in his career, Benedict XVI will encapsulate and consecrate the modernism of the new religion of Rome with the beatification and perhaps one day canonization of John Paul II as a saint. This, of course, would be in keeping right order. John Paul II is the *"saint"* of the new religion of Rome masquerading as Catholicism.

Second Edition Update: Since the first publication of this book, Benedict XVI stepped down on February 28, 2013. Argentina's Jorge Mario Bergoglio was elected today March 13, 2013 and took the name Francis I. Based on his background evolvement of ecumenical worship services with Jews; it appears that the great apostasy rolls on.

The Implications

Rome has been without a true pope for over fifty years with a dim future for one in sight. The last six claimants have been antipopes and usurpers to the papal throne.

Because Roncalli and Montini became members of a secret society (also another religion), both of them were automatically excommunicated by both Divine law and Church law; Canon 2335.

Roncalli's election should be considered null and void and his promotion of Montini to the cardinalate invalid. All successive promotions to the cardinalate would also be invalid such as Luciani's, Wojtyla's, Ratzinger's, and now Bergoglio's.

All six claimants to the throne were never true popes as all of their elections were invalid. None of them were ever Catholic after 1958 A.D. All of them began as antipopes and died as antipopes for the exception of the current living antipope emeritus Ratzinger, and Bergoglio.

Therefore, the Second Vatican Council is a robber council and totally invalid. All the new teachings, decrees, laws, and practices that stem from the time of Roncalli are to be considered null and void. All the novelties are illicit and many of them are completely invalid. The new mass is an abomination because a true sacrifice is absent. Because the new rite of orders of priests and bishops are invalid, the capability to confect the Eucharist and absolve sins is no longer conferred.

Even if John Paul II or Ratzinger were true popes, their acts of apostasy would have automatically disqualified them.

We'll see what Bergoglio will do, but for now we must presume that he's just another secular head of state only until the contrary is proven.

However, if he, in fact, manifestly retracts all errors of the conciliar popes, he could assume the papal office despite the fact that he was elected by invalid cardinals. As we've seen in history, antipopes have assumed the office of pope without ever having a lawful election. One of those popes is a saint in the Church.

There would be no reason to reject an unlawfully elected pope if he's universally recognized as a claimant to the papacy with the historic Catholic Faith and manifestly rejects all the nonsense before him.

In a nutshell, Rome has apostatized and replaced Catholicism with a new modernist Masonic religion in its place. The name Catholic has been usurped. All followers who know and understand the situation and remain united to Rome are automatically outside of the Church.

The true Catholic Church is a small left-over remnant who holds fast to all historic Catholic teachings and practices.

The apologists of modernist Rome today will argue in defense of the very teachings and acts of the last fifty years because they hold to two main positions. First, they believe heretics can be popes until declared otherwise as they will twist canon laws to make that point. Secondly, they don't care what is taught or done by their *"popes"* because nothing will deter them from recognizing the obvious fact that Rome has apostatized.

The same apologists will argue against the position of sedevacantism by saying that mere laymen don't have the authority to declare a pope as an antipope. The fact is no one has that authority. However, all Catholics have the authority to declare an antipope as an antipope.

The promise of Christ that the gates of hell shall not prevail would be false if the last six claimants were true popes.

The gates of hell are heretics and their heresies according to the Catholic Church.

Pope Leo XIII called the Roman Pontiffs *"the Gates of the Church"* in his 1894 A.D. encyclical letter *Praeclara gratulationis publicae*.

Therefore, the *"Gates of the Church"* cannot be one and the same as the *"gates of hell."*

We know that the Church does not exist for the sake of the papacy or the rest of the hierarchy, but rather, it is the hierarchy that exists for the sake of the Church.

We have seen in history Catholics living for centuries without any hierarchy. Japan is a prime example. The Church can and will survive till the very end. This is the promise of Our Lord.

The Great Apostasy foretold in Scripture will surely be disastrous, and it happens around the time of the final antichrist just before the Second Coming.

Christ said, *"I tell you that he will avenge them quickly. Yet when the Son of Man comes, will he find, do you think, faith on the earth?"* (Luke 18:8)

It would appear that He was emphasizing that Day will be so bad that very few will actually profess the true faith. Christ never promised a pope in every generation. When He built the Church on Peter, it was on him and his faith. The Church has never stated otherwise. All of Peter's successors must be in union with Christ, Peter, and Peter's Faith to be part of the Church.

Christ also taught, *"But of that day and hour no one knows, not even the angels of heaven, nor the Son, but the Father only. As were the days of Noah, so will be the coming of the Son of man. For as in those days before the flood they were eating and drinking, marrying and giving in marriage, until the day when Noah entered the ark, and they did not know until the flood came and swept them all away, so will be the coming of the Son of man."* (Matt. 24:36-39)

In other words, Our Lord was saying that everything will seem honky-dory, but in reality, the world will be without the true faith even though professing to have it. The end will come and all will be lost for those not in the Ark, which symbolizes the historic Catholic Church.

A Summary of Implications:
From the Twenty Anomalies

The Catholic Church can remain unified without a pope for many years. The absence of a pope does not contradict the dogma of the First Vatican Council that St. Peter has perpetual successors. The perpetual principle and visible foundation remains without a pope during long interregnums even when the Church is underground.

The Church has not determined if certain claimants to the papal throne are valid or invalid. It is left up to the opinion of theologians and the faithful. They have recognized true popes as antipopes, and have recognized antipopes or doubtful popes as true popes. Great popes and saints are included as those faithful who recognized them incorrectly.

The Church has recognized popes who were unlawfully elected and began as antipopes.

The Church has recognized popes who were never elected.

The Church has recognized that a true pope can become a heretic making him an antipope. In the case of Honorius, saints and true popes have recognized that another true pope can become a heretic over an undefined doctrine; another astounding fact within the ranks of Catholicism.

The church at Rome has been in schism more than once, by recognizing invalid deposals of true popes and then recognizing their invalid replacements.

The Church doesn't always recognize Divine or Church law. Simony has not always been recognized as a nullifying factor in the election of popes when the ecclesiastical law specified it.

The law that required a consecration before being recognized as the Roman Pontiff was either ignored or rejected by Church theologians without censor.

The Church does recognize layman popes and historically recognized a pope who remained a layman.

The Church has held an antipope as the true pope. The official papal list demonstrates that throughout history, the Church has changed its view on who has been valid and who has not. The Church can go many years not knowing who the true pope is thus demonstrating that the Church can function to some extent (if not correctly or completely) indefinitely without a pope since doubtful popes are the equivalent to an antipope or vacancy (no pope at all).

The Church recognized (incorrectly) that a child could become the pope.

Sometimes the Church doesn't seem to care who are the true popes or antipopes as no explanation is ever given, perhaps because it doesn't affect the Church.

The majority doesn't always determine who the true pope is. The minority has made the correct decision.

Popes can err concerning doctrine provided that they have not contradicted defined doctrine and the error itself is not universally formal.

It is possible to have another true pope outside of any Church law since it has happened already in history.

The last anomaly implies that the Church can exist for over fifty years without a true pope and antipope usurpers.

Perhaps the greatest anomaly of all is the fact that the Church has never defined what makes a pope a pope. It has always been assumed. Again, the Church has recognized valid popes who were never elected, or invalidly, unlawfully and unjustly elected, and who were recognized by the minority rather than the majority. The only thing that the Church is clear about is the fact that a woman and a heretic/apostate/schismatic/non-Catholic cannot be the pope. True popes can be evil, but that can't be non-Catholic.

Author's List of Popes and Antipopes

> ➢ Unlawfully elected – antipopes in the beginning.

> * Questionable (not necessarily doubtful).

> XXX Unholy via immoral, unchaste, murder, mercilessness, cruelty, or worldliness (only notorious popes listed - definite antipopes excluded).

> < > Relinquished their pontificate, unless they are marked as a questionable (several questionable popes, in fact, relinquished the office).

> *Italics* Definite antipopes placed off to the right side in brackets at the approximate time as the true pope.

The popes:

First Century

St. Peter – Dante mentions him in fourteen cantos of *"The Divine Comedy."*
St. Linus – Dante mentions him once.
St. Anacletus (also known as Cletus) – Dante: once
St. Clement
St. Evaristus (97 to 105 A.D)

Second Century

St. Alexander I
St. Sixtus I – Dante: once
St. Telesphorus
St. Hyginus

St. Pius I – Dante: once
St. Anicetus
St. Soter
St. Eleutherius
St. Victor I
St. Zephyrinus (99 to 217 A.D)   [*Natalius*]

Third Century

St. Callistus I – Dante: once   [*St. Hippolytus*]
St. Urban I – Dante: once
<St. Pontian> – First to pope to abdicate.
St. Anterus
St. Fabian
St. Cornelius   [*Novatian*]
St. Lucius I
St. Stephen I
St. Sixtus II
St. Dionysius
St. Felix I
St. Eutychian
St. Caius
St. Marcellinus (296 to 304 A.D.)

Fourth Century

St. Marcellus I
St. Eusebius
St. Melchiades
St. Sylvester I – Due to the forged document of the Middle Ages
             known as the *Donation of Constantine*, Dante
             placed him in hell.
St. Mark
St. Julius I
Liberius* – began legitimately and became doubtful – See p. 33
St. Felix II* – See p. 33
Damasus   [*Ursinus*]

St. Siricius
St. Anastasius I (399 to 401 A.D.)

Fifth Century

St. Innocent I
St. Zozimus
St. Boniface I [*Eulalius*]
St. Celestine I
St. Sixtus III
St. Leo the Great
St. Hilary
St. Simplicius
St. Felix III
St. Gelasius I
Anastasius II – Due to historic mix-up, Dante placed him in hell.
St. Symmachus (498 to 514 A.D.) [*Lawrence*]

Sixth Century

St. Hormisdas
St. John I
St. Felix IV
  ➢ XXX Boniface II* – mercilessness
Dioscorus* – See p. 43
John II
St. Agapetus I – Dante: once
St. Silverius
  ➢ XXX Vigilius – See p. 47
Pelagius I
John III
Benedict I
Pelagius II
St. Gregory the Great (590 to 604 A.D.) – Dante: thrice

Seventh Century

Sabinian
Boniface III
Boniface IV
St. Deusdedit (Also known as Adeodatus I)
Boniface V
Honorius I – began legitimately and became doubtful – See p. 53
Severinus
John IV
Theodore I
> St. Martin I <
 ➢ St. Eugene I – See p. 59
St. Vitalian
Deusdedit (Also known as Adeodatus II)
Donus
St. Agatho
St. Leo II
St. Benedict II
John V
Conon   [*Theodore, Paschal*]
St. Sergius I (687 to 701 A.D.)

Eighth Century

John VI
John VII
Sisinnius
Constantine
St. Gregory II
St. Gregory III
St. Zachary
Stephen (II)* – See p. 65
Stephen II
St. Paul I   [*Constantine, Philip*]
   XXX Stephen III – mercilessness

Hadrian I
St. Leo III (795 to 816 A.D.)

Ninth Century

Stephen IV
St. Paschal I
Eugene II
Valentine
Gregory IV [*John VIII*]
Sergius II
St. Leo IV
Benedict III [*Anastasius*]
St. Nicholas I
Hadrian II
John VIII
Marinus I (also known as Martin II)
St. Hadrian III
Stephen V
Formosus
        XXX Boniface VI* – See p. 69
        XXX Stephen VI* – See p. 69
Romanus
Theodore II
John IX
Benedict IV (900 to 903 A.D.)

Tenth Century

Leo V [*Christopher*]
        XXX Sergius III – See p. 74
Anastasius III
Lando
John X
Leo VI* – See p. 73
Stephen VII* – See p. 73
John XI

Leo VII
Stephen VIII
Marinus II (also known as Martin III)
Agapetus II
        XXX John XII* – See p. 79 for explanation for the next two *'s
Leo VIII*
Benedict V*
John XIII
Benedict VI   [*Boniface VII*]
Benedict VII
John XIV
        XXX Boniface VII* – See p. 85
John XV
Gregory V   [*John XVI*]
Sylvester II (999 to 1003 A.D.)

Eleventh Century

John XVII
John XVIII
Sergius IV
Benedict VIII   [*Gregory*]
John XIX
        XXX Benedict IX* – See p. 89 for explanation for the next five *'s
Sylvester III*
Benedict IX (second term)*
Gregory VI*
Clement II
Benedict IX (third term)*
Damasus II*
St. Leo IX
Victor II
Stephen IX   [*Benedict X*] – See p. 95
Nicholas II
Alexander II   [*Honorius II*]
St. Gregory VII   [*Clement III*]

Bl. Victor III
Bl. Urban II
Paschal II (1099 to 1118 A.D.)   [*Theoderic, Albert, Sylvester IV*]

Twelfth Century

Gelasius II   [*Gregory VIII*]
Callistus II
Honorius II   [*Celestine II*]
Innocent II   [*Anacletus II, Victor IV*]
Celestine II
Lucius II
Eugene III
Anastasius
Hadrian IV
Alexander III   [*Victor IV, Paschal III,
                            Callistus III, Innocent III*]

Lucius III
Urban III
Gregory VIII
Clement III
Celestine III
Innocent III (1198 to 1216 A.D.) – Dante: once

Thirteenth Century

Honorius III – Dante: twice
Gregory IX
Celestine IV
Innocent IV
Alexander IV
Urban IV
Clement IV – Dante: once
Bl. Gregory X
Bl. Innocent V
Hadrian V* – See p. 111 – Dante placed him in purgatory for avarice.

John XXI – Dante placed him in heaven. (There was no John XX and technically there were only eighteen popes who had legitimately possessed the papacy. Not all popes assigned themselves numbers but this John selected the number *XXI* for himself. He apparently miscounted or included antipopes as the explanation for the numbering. There are several anomalies associated with the numbering of popes such as an antipope's number being reused or rejected.)

Nicholas III – Dante placed him in hell for simony.
Martin IV – Dante placed him in purgatory for gluttony. Martin died from eating too many eels from the lake of Bolsena, stewed in Vernaccia wine.
Honorius IV
Nicholas IV
> St. Celestine V< – Dante placed him in hell for quitting
    XXX Boniface VIII (1284 to 1303 A.D.) – murder – p. 91 – Dante placed him in hell for simony and mentions him in twelve cantos.

Fourteenth Century

Benedict XI
Clement V* – Dante placed him in hell
John XXII – Dante: once   [*Nicholas V*]
Benedict XII
Clement VI
Innocent VI
Bl. Urban V
Gregory XI
    XXX Urban VI* – See p. 119 for explanation for the next five *'s
Boniface IX* (1389 to 1404 A.D.)

Fifteenth Century

Innocent VII*
Gregory XII *
Clement VII*
Benedict XIII*　　　　　[*Alexander V, John XXIII*]
Clement VIII*　　　　　[*Two Benedict XIV's (Bernard*
Martin V　　　　　　　　*Garnier and Jean Carrier)*]
Eugene IV　　　　　　　[*Felix V*]
Nicholas V
Callistus III
Pius II
Paul II

　　　　XXX Sixtus IV – immoral and worldly
　　　　XXX Innocent VIII – worldly
　　　　XXX Alexander VI* (1492 to 1503 A.D.) – See p. 129

Sixteenth Century

Pius III
　　　　XXX Julius II – immoral and worldly
　　　　XXX Leo X – worldly
Hadrian VI
　　　　XXX Clement VII* – See pp. 134
　　　　XXX Paul III – unchaste and worldly
Julius III
Marcellus II
Paul IV
Pius IV
St. Pius V
Gregory XIII
Sixtus V
Urban VII
Gregory XIV
Innocent IX
Clement VIII (1592 to 1605 A.D.)

Seventeenth Century

Leo XI
Paul V
Gregory XV
Urban VIII
Innocent X
Alexander VII
Clement IX
Clement X
Bl. Innocent XI
Alexander VIII
Innocent XII
Clement XI (1700 to 1721 A.D.)

Eighteenth Century

Innocent XIII
Benedict XIII
Clement XII
Benedict XIV
Clement XIII
Clement XIV
Pius VI
Pius VII (1800 to 1823 A.D.)

Nineteenth Century

Leo XII
Pius VIII
Gregory XVI
Pius IX
Leo XIII (1878 to 1903 A.D.)

Twentieth Century

St. Pius X
Benedict XV
Pius XI
Pius XII

[*John XXIII, Paul VI, John Paul I, John Paul II* (1978 to 2005 A.D.)]

Twenty First Century

[*Benedict XVI, Francis I*]

Conclusions

There have been at least forty-five definite antipopes and thirty possible antipopes (counting Benedict IX thrice and Honorius becoming so, excluding Stephen II and Hadrian V) rounding off the total at seventy-five.

At least eighteen claimants have been unholy popes (excluding definite antipopes) if you include Benedict IX thrice.

Dante specified twenty-two popes in his Divine Comedy: Six are in hell; two are in purgatory; twelve are in heaven, leaving two that are mentioned in passing.

For the first time in Christian history, a century exists without claiming a true pope.

Bibliography

Arriaga, Joaquin Saenz y, *The New Montinian Church*. Edgar A. Lucidi, 1985 A.D.

Belloc, Hilaire, *The Crusades*. TAN Books and Publishers, INC., Rockford, Illinois, republished 1992 A.D.

Catholic Encyclopedia, Encyclopedia Press, New York, 1912 A.D.

Carrol, Warren H., *The Building of Christendom*. Christendom College Press, Front Royal, Virginia, 1987 A.D.

The Glory of Christendom. Christendom College Press, Front Royal, Virginia, 1993 A.D.

Chamberlin, Eric R. *The Bad Popes*. Dial Press, New York, 1969 A.D.

Coomaraswamy, Rama P., *The Destruction of the Christian Tradition*. World Wisdom, 2006 A.D.

Dante Alighieri, *Dante: The Divine Comedy*. Translated by Charles Bagot Cayley (1823–1883), BiblioBazaar, 2009 A.D.

Decrees of the Ecumenical Councils. Volume I – Sheed and Ward and Georgetown University Press, 1990 A.D.

Decrees of the Ecumenical Councils. Volume II – Sheed and Ward and Georgetown University Press, 1990 A.D.

Fellows, Mark, *Fatima in Twilight*. Marmion Publications, Niagara Falls, NY, 2003 A.D.

Hollis, Christopher, *The Papacy*. The Macmillan Company, New York, 1964 A.D.

Kelly, J.N.D., *The Oxford Dictionary of Popes*. Oxford University Press, 1986 A.D.

Madrid, Patrick, *Pope Fiction*. Basilica Press, San Diego, 1999 A.D.

Mann, Horace, *The Lives of the Popes in the Middle Ages*. Kegan Paul, Trench, Trubner and Co., London, 1932 A.D.

Martin, Malachi, *The Decline and Fall of the Roman Church*. G.P. Putnam's Sons, New York, 1981 A.D.

The Jesuits - The Society of Jesus and the Betrayal of the Roman Catholic Church, Simon & Schuster, New York, 1987 A.D.

McBrien, Richard P., *The Lives of the Popes. : The Pontiffs from St. Peter to Benedict XVI.* HarperCollins Publishers, New York, 1997 A.D.

Ott, Ludwig, *Fundamentals of Catholic Dogma*. TAN Books and Publishers, INC., Rockford, Illinois, 1974 A.D.

Packard, Jerrold M., *Peter's Kingdom*. Charles Scribner's Sons, New York, 1985 A.D.

Pastor, Ludwig (Freiherr von), *The History of Popes from the Close of the Middle Ages* – Volume Six – Second Edition. B. Herder 17 S. Broadway, St. Louis, Missouri, 1901 A.D.

Pontifical Yearbook *(Annuario Pontificio)*, Libreria Editrice Vaticano, Vatican City, 1869 A.D. and other editions.

Schimmelpfennig, Bernhard, *The Papacy*. Columbia University Press, New York, Oxford, 1992 A.D.

Shouppe, F.X., *Purgatory Explained by the Lives and Legends of the Saints*. TAN Books and Publishers, INC., Rockford, Illinois, republished 2006 A.D.

Speray, Steven, *The Greatest Conspiracy Ever*. Confiteor, Versailles, KY, 2009 A.D.

The 1917 Pio-Benedictine Code of Canon Law. Edward N. Peters, Ignatius Press, San Francisco, 2001 A.D.

The Book of Pontiffs (Liber Pontificalis). Raymond Davis, Liverpool University Press, 2000

The Book of Popes (Liber Pontificalis). Louise Ropes Loomis, Columbia University Press, New York, 1916 A.D.

The Sources of Catholic Dogma. Denzinger "Enchiridion Symbolorum", Roy J. Deferrari, 13th Edition, Loreto Publications, 1954 A.D.

Young, Norwood, *The Story of Rome*. J.M. Dent, London, 1901 A.D.

ABOUT THE AUTHOR

Steven Brian Speray resides in Versailles, Kentucky with his wife and three children.

His training was in Strategic Weapons Systems (Submarine Ballistic Missiles) of the U.S. Navy.

He has worked as a Catholic apologist writing, teaching, and giving lectures on the Catholic Faith.

Steven has authored several books on the Catholic Church, such as:

- Baptism of Desire or Blood (A Defense in Brief, Ad Majorem Dei Gloriam)

- Catholicism in a Nutshell

- The Greatest Conspiracy Ever

- The Key to the Apocalypse

- Debunking Sedevacantism?

- The New Church of Rome VS The Ancient Church of Rome – Forty Differences

- Latitudinarian Maxims – The Divine Law on Catholic Communication in Religion with Non-Catholics Contrasting the Past with the Present

Steven is an avid weightlifter and swimmer, and a retired boxer (undefeated). You may find him playing tennis with his brothers, or chopping wood for the winter.

www.ingramcontent.com/pod-product-compliance
Lightning Source LLC
Chambersburg PA
CBHW020802160426

43192CB00006B/410